Spiritual Bathing

Spiritual Bathing

Healing Rituals and Traditions
from Around the World

Rosita Arvigo and Nadine Epstein

LOCATION PHOTOGRAPHY BY Thayer Allyson Gowdy

Celestial Arts
Berkeley | Toronto

To our children and their children

A Kirsty Melville Book

Celestial Arts
P.O. Box 7123
Berkeley, California
94707

Distributed in Australia by Simon and Schuster Australia, in Canada by Ten Speed Press Canada, in New Zealand by Southern Publishers Group, in South Africa by Real Books, and in the United Kingdom and Europe by Airlift Book Company.

Cover and book design by Nancy Austin

Library of Congress Cataloging-in-Publication Data

Arvigo, Rosita.
  Spiritual bathing : healing rituals and traditions from around the world / Rosita Arvigo and Nadine Epstein ; photography by Thayer Allyson Gowdy.
      p. cm.
"A Kirsty Melville Book."
Includes bibliographical references.
  ISBN 1-58761-170-8
  1. Water--Religious aspects. 2. Water--Folklore. 3. Bathing customs--Religious aspects. 4. Purity, Ritual. I. Epstein, Nadine. II. Title.
BL450 .A78 2003
291.4'46--dc21
                              2003013313

First printing, 2003

Printed in Singapore
1 2 3 4 5 6 7 8 9 10 - 06 05 04 03

Acknowledgments

We would like to thank the late Mircea Eliade, professor of comparative religion at the University of Chicago, and others like him—who were navigating through the vast sea of human traditions and culture before we were born. This includes inspirational healers, collectors, and teachers of folk knowledge we have been fortunate to meet such as the late Don Elijio Panti, Hortence Robinson, Beatrice Waight, Teresa Leal, Anita Diamant, and James Bronson.

The staffs of the Library of Congress and D.C. Public Libraries deserve our gratitude, especially those at the Chevy Chase and Cleveland Park branches. Researcher Christina Pepper and art historian Betty Stoller provided invaluable support. Monica Bussolati gave generously of her time and was instrumental in this undertaking from the very beginning.

Caroline Kenner, Elieen Dzik, and Margaret Beatty read the entire manuscript. Rabbi Miriam Berkowitz, Vance Whitesides, Andrea Carlson, Pam Roe, Debra St. Clair, Raaj Sah, Ben Biber, Michael Balick, Jim Jamohammad, and others provided essential comments. Maria Lasa Sloan of the Adas Israel Congregation in Washington D.C., Zeny Harris, Jessica Barnes, Ephim Schluger, Mark Green, and Rebecca Frankel gave generously of their time.

We couldn't have written this book without the support and love of family and friends, including Ruth and Seymour Epstein, Michael Epstein, Marcy Epstein and Barbara Ohrstrom, Mildred Epstein, Donald and Jeanne Epstein and family, John O'Leary, Linda Feldmann, Eileen Dzik, Lisa Newman, Terry Hong, Debra Bruno, and Jan Genzer.

We are proud of Sam Yalda for bravely taking on the challenge of writing for the first time.

This book is dedicated to our children—Noah, Jimmy, Jimmy, and Crystal—to whom we are grateful for so much. Thank you for your kind patience. A special thanks to Noah Phillips, who had to share his Mom with the book on a daily basis, and to Jimmy Arvigo, who held down the fort in Belize while his mother was away.

Contents

Authors' Note

We have gathered together ancient and contemporary spiritual baths spanning six continents, from the rituals of the Maya to the Mikvah and the Great Kumbh Mela. Some traditions were buried in books; others are practiced regularly in faraway lands or just down the street—in churches, synagogues, mosques, temples of all kinds, spas, and storefronts.

We offer you our findings. As you might guess, our task of coalescing knowledge and rituals turned out to be considerably greater than we originally imagined. We regret that we were not able to include every culture and tradition that deserves to be in this book. And we recognize that spiritual bathing, so closely tied with religion and deeply felt beliefs, can be a delicate subject; if we have inadvertently offended anyone, we apologize. This book is our interpretation, one that we hope will be helpful to contemporary readers.

Our quest to understand spiritual bathing is truly a work in process, so we are grateful for your ideas and suggestions. We would love to hear from you through our website at www.spiritualbathing.com.

Rosita Arvigo, San Ignacio, Belize
Nadine Epstein, Washington, D.C.
2003

Introduction

Spiritual bathing draws men, women, children, and whole communities closer to the Divine. Perhaps the best-known practice is immersion, which expresses rebirth, regeneration, and momentary death. "Immersion is the equivalent, at the human level, of death at the cosmic level, of the cataclysm (the Flood) which periodically dissolves the world into primeval ocean," wrote Mircea Eliade. "Breaking up all forms, doing away with the past, water possesses the power of purifying, of regenerating, of giving new birth. Water purifies and regenerates because it nullifies the past, and restores—even if only for a moment—the integrity of the dawn of things."

"A daily spiritual bath is an easy way to start paying attention to your spirit and soul as well as your body."

—TIERAONA LOW DOG, M.D.

But immersion is only one spiritual bathing act; sprinkling, splashing, pouring, sweating, and even drinking are equally important. All of these acts call upon the powers of water, whether liquid or vapor; prayer; occasionally honey, milk, or wine, and even plants and gems.

At a time when each of us is seeking our own path toward an individual relationship with God, spiritual baths are more meaningful than ever. As we bustle through over-scheduled lives, we need as many ways as possible to regain our sense of interconnectedness and to feel harmony within and without. Spiritual bathing strengthens our tenuous connection with the natural world and its reflection of the divine. It separates us from the mundane, transporting us to a holier place; it eases our passage through the stresses of daily life, opening the door to our soul's inner guidance; it marks rites of passage; and it uplifts the soul, fostering a reverent, peaceful state of mind.

Opposite: *Day of the Gods (Mahana No Atua)*, 1894, Paul Gauguin (1848–1903). Oil on canvas, 26 x 36 inches, Helen Birch-Bartlett Memorial Collection.

Although it has religious roots, spiritual bathing is not necessarily about religion or being part of a particular community or institution, although it can be. Contemporary spiritual bathing can and does take place outside the context of organized religion, and it transcends any one tradition by incorporating various ideas and rituals. To reshape rituals for modern times and create new ones, we need to deepen our understanding of the old traditions. Spiritual bathing can be a private experience or adapted for use with friends and family, and can be practiced at home in the backyard or by a natural body of water such as a sea, lake, river, spring, or pond. It is often incorporated into healing practices throughout the world.

Common Threads of the World's Spiritual Bathing Traditions

~ Water is sacred and can cleanse and purify the spirit.

~ Spiritual baths separate the mundane from the spiritual and are often preludes to religious ceremonies.

~ Spiritual baths help people open to spiritual guidance and the wisdom and beauty of Nature and the Divine.

~ Spiritual baths often mark rites of passage.

~ Spiritual bathing removes negative influences and protects people from them.

~ Ritual baths are used to purify votive statues and idols.

~ Holy or "lustral" water is produced by praying over water.

A Few Words About Spiritual Bathing

ablution (from Latin *abluere*) To wash away; the washing of one's body or part of it as a religious act.

aspersion (from Latin *aspersus*) To scatter and to sprinkle with water.

immersion (from Latin *immersus*) To merge or plunge into something that surrounds or covers.

libation (from Latin *libare*) To pour out as an offering.

lustration (from Latin *lustrare*) To brighten or purify or to purify ceremonially.

purification (from Latin *purus*) To cleanse; the act of being purified.

Why Spiritual Bathing Practices in the Western World Went into Decline

We believe that spiritual bathing in the West is on the verge of a new renaissance. Two thousand years ago, the Greco-Roman public bath drew millions of people; pagans, Jews, early Christians, Mandaeans, and others openly practiced ritual bathing. Under the increasingly austere influence of the medieval Roman Catholic church these vibrant, living spiritual bathing traditions were forced underground. Any ritual that included nudity or mixed-gender bathing was stamped out, as was anything considered a threat to church authority. Bathhouses and holy wells were replaced by churches and shrines; practitioners of water- and earth-based spirituality were hunted down and punished.

In a fluke of history, Christians began to equate physical dirtiness with religious fervor and penance for sins. Religious belief spilled over into science, and for many centuries people considered any kind of bathing for any purpose unhygienic. Even royalty frowned upon bathing.

Fortunately, spiritual bathing survived intact in Asia, although some traditions were influenced by Western definitions of morality. And many indigenous peoples—including those of the Americas and Africa—managed to defy missionaries by incorporating their spiritual bathing practices into Christianity.

Eventually, it was the influence of the East that softened the anti-bathing attitudes of Europeans. Englishmen returning from India and the Ottoman Empire became accustomed to the benefits of regular bathing long before the germ theory came along to support the idea of washing to remove harmful bacteria.

Nevertheless, as the church's influence waned, new phenomena undermined spiritual ritual of all kinds. Descartes' separation of mind and body transformed the western concept of healing. The Rationalists led western peoples away from mystery, and the rise of science drove them to reject "quaint folk customs." Far too many spiritual bathing rituals were thrown onto the trash heap of "superstition." Fortunately for us, scavengers of spiritual rituals have now begun to reappreciate what remains.

A spiritual bath usually combines water, prayer, and ritual—and sometimes includes plants—to wash away the negative effects of:

• Anger

• Fear and anxiety

• Grief and trauma

• Exhaustion and world-weariness

• Confusion and disquietude

• A broken heart

• Unwanted and harmful emotional baggage

• Stress

It is a healing practice that anyone can learn to do, either in the privacy of his or her own home or in a group setting. People who take or receive spiritual baths have experienced remarkable healing transformations.

The Components of Spiritual Bathing

Divine Water and Life on the Earth

In ancient times, when travelers came to a river, they drank and gave thanks to the life-giving energy of the waters that sustained them. The flowing water evoked a sense of wonder at the inherent magic of the world and reminded each of them of their connection to the Divine. They knew that they owed their existence to the natural forces around them, and that they were but a thread in the mysterious web of life.

These travelers, resting for a moment on the riverbank, knew something that we have mostly forgotten. We know it is refreshing to immerse and drench ourselves in water, and we are generally aware of its therapeutic value. Yet most of us have lost touch with our spiritual relationship to water.

Until recently, water was one of the most universal spiritual concepts on our planet. Buried somewhere in the genesis of every culture is the idea that water is divine, life-giving, healing, cleansing, and renewing. Some people even considered water to be a living being.

Divine or not, water is the enabler of life, the *élan vital* of our planet and the precondition for its blossoming. Some life forms at the bottom of the seas can exist without light, but no life can survive without water.

"Dispenser of life, water is the manifestation of the Divine spirit itself."

—MIRCEA ELIADE

The sacred spiritual bath always includes water and prayer, and sometimes flowers or plants.

Water is the universal solvent that delivers the stuff of life to all living forms. Every lake, stream, river, and ocean is a solution containing thousands of substances in ionic form, such as metals, non-metals, and organic and inorganic compounds. When you hold a glass of water up to the light it looks clear, yet it is actually laden with charged particles, dancing around each other in an invisible chemical ballet of magnesium, calcium, phosphorus, and myriad natural and essential substances.

Water and the Human Body

Every human being has an inner and outer relationship with water. The amniotic fluid in our mother's womb was our first bath. The first living cells were formed in the salt bath of the sea and our bloodstream is much like seawater. The life functions formerly served by the sea are now carried on by the tissue fluids—the blood, lymph, and other liquids that flow through and around our cells. Every living cell has a fluid interior surrounded by a solution of various substances dissolved in water. Water is the only solvent in our bodies since we were made to interact with the rest of the universe.

As we often hear, we are mostly water. Our bodies are 85% water. The kidneys are 82% water; the muscles, 75% water; the liver, 69% water; even the bones are 22% water. Water makes up nine tenths of our blood, saliva, plasma, lymph, urine, synovial fluid of the joints, and the cerebrospinal fluid. Our watery blood carries nutrients, hormones, proteins, and chemical messengers to help us to stay afloat in the sea of life. All of the waste in the body is dissolved and eliminated by water. Water, the great solvent, is also the primary transporter of oxygen to our cells, and maintains the exact acid and alkaline balance that, if only slightly awry, brings about illness in a very short time.

Water and Civilization

In the beginning there was only water. Such is the story with which most cultures explained the first moment of creation. When water was separated from chaos, land, life, and even gods came forth. Form, order, and civilization emerged from turbulent seas.

Almost every ancient civilization thought that life began in the sea. The sea represents infinity, the cosmic ocean from which all life sprang and into which it must eventually dissolve and return.

The word for sea in most languages is feminine and is connected with the feminine creative principle. Many ancients considered it to be the "juice of the earth's womb."[1] The Sumerians used the same word, *mar,* for sea and womb. This word gradually morphed into the name *Mary,* the root of Virgin Mary, marriage, marital, and maritime.

The early Sumerians considered water the primordial element that came from an abyss that surrounded the earth. They personified water as Apsu and Tiamet, and later Enki, the creator of life-giving streams, rivers, and lakes. The Persians deified the goddess Anahita, whose fertilizing waters poured down from the earth, giving fecundity to all.[2] The Yoruba goddess Obatala created the world from a floating ball of water. Vishnu in India formed the earth while he floated on a serpent in the cosmic seas. In Native American myths, the earth lay still and barren until Old Man appeared, floating on a raft, and willed the earth into existence out of the water.

Children of the primordial waters were the rivers, symbols of fertility and the never-ending flow of time and energy. People's interactions with rivers constitute much of the history of civilization. The Tigris and Euphrates of Mesopotamia, the Ganges of India, the Hwang Ho or Yellow River of China, and the Nile are among the rivers that have spawned mighty civilizations, their waters enabling agriculture and trade to flourish. The Egyptians even invented the 365-day calendar to coincide with the annual flooding of the Nile.

The sacredness of water is not confined to seas and rivers. Cultures around the globe have designated lakes, rivers, ponds, and grottoes as sacred sites thought to embody the manifestation of the Divine. Native Americans, Celts, and others believed that springs were living entities, points where creation came to the surface and spilled out, where a human hand could actually reach out and feel the emergence of the divine.

"God created the heaven and the earth. The earth was without form and void, and darkness was upon the face of the deep; and the spirit of God was moving over the face of the waters."

—GENESIS

The Worship of Water

Some ancients worshiped water, air, fire, and earth; others, like the Chinese, revered wood, wind, fire, metal, and water. The sun and the moon were also worshiped. These were divine forces of nature that orchestrated the seasons and cycles of flooding.

We humans have spent thousands of years conceiving of gods, goddesses, nymphs, sprites, and undines that inhabit and guard water. Our world is flooded with stories of water gods and mythical water creatures, some of whom dwell in places now considered sacred. These supernatural beings have long helped us to express our beliefs about water as well as our confusion and fears.

Water can be both divine architect and demonic destroyer, just like the gods and goddesses who represent it. The Chinese feared the ocean; like many other cultures, they saw the sea as populated by dangerous, menacing spirits that had to be appeased and respected. Dire consequences befell those who ignored the spirits. The Maya water goddess Ix Chel could heal or destroy, much like the Sumerian Tiamet. Russian peasants believed in *vanodynes*—intrinsically greedy, evil spirits known to devour the unwary who lolled lazily on river shores. The Zulus thought it unwise to look into water, as this would call forth a beast that sustained itself by stealing human souls. A Chinese proverb says simply and profoundly, "Water floats a ship. Water sinks a ship."

The Soothing, Spiritual Presence of Water

"The reflective talents of water have given life to many a landscape."

—CARL A. KOENIG

Siddhartha, who became the Buddha, attained enlightenment as he meditated by the river's edge and heard the gurgle of water passing over the rocks, whispering to him of the oneness of all life.

One of the easiest ways to attain a sense of peace and contentment is through silent, contemplative water meditation, at any time of day and at any water site. As we sit and gaze at the reflection of the rising and setting sun or the brilliance of moonlight reflected on restless waves, the dancing play of color-infused light and water is spellbinding, focusing us on beauty and harmony instead of on our troubles. The sounds of water, wherever they are, are also powerful: The crashing and breaking of ocean waves or the babbling of a stream is a comforting, sleep-inducing sound. The sound of rain upon the roof creates a sense of peace and security.

The Energy of Water

Nearly all religions and cultures equate water with energy. Hindus revere water as liquid energy. The Shinto believe that water remembers and carries with it vibratory patterns of the sun's energy, the phases of the moon, and other patterns of nature. The energy accumulated by water running through mountain streams carries the memory of fresh pure air and light to creeks and rivers in the valleys below. The Incas designed their temples so that the accumulated spiritual energy of water flowing from the sacred city Machu Picchu reached the ceremonial sites and villages below.

Since ancient times people have firmly believed that the energy carried by water can transform human energy. This is central to the understanding of the effect of spiritual bathing on the human body.

What is it about this noblest of all elements, so unique and so common, that allows it to be universally healing to body, mind, and soul? According to biologists and physicists, water's molecular structure is the key. Water consist of two gases, oxygen and hydrogen, that when combined form a liquid. This can be easily changed to vapor by heating and to a solid by freezing.

Molecules vibrate, whirl, and dart, making and breaking bonds with electric speed. The bonding of hydrogen and oxygen is what makes water the universal solvent of substances and energy. The hydrogen bond with oxygen is electrostatic in nature, restless and never in repose. The oxygen atom has two unpaired electrons, which is an unstable state in nature. Therefore, the water molecule is eager to attract another atomic substance. It wants a partner and will happily, eagerly reach out for a relationship, then try its best to hold on. Imagine a "lonely bonds" ad in the classifieds that reads, "Water molecule, strong, unique, fun-loving, energetic, and spiritually oriented, seeks to bond with anyone and anything for short- or long-term relationship."

Hydrogen molecules are present in almost every substance on the earth, and they can't resist bonding with water molecules. Why does hydrogen prefer water? Every molecule has an electric charge. Oxygen has a positive charge and hydrogen has a negative charge. The positive charge in one oxygen atom is four times stronger than the positive charge in two hydrogen atoms. As a result, the marriage between one hydrogen and one water molecule can create four molecular bonds.

This means that water can easily bond with all elements that possess a hydrogen molecule. Fortunately for water, almost everything on earth has hydrogen in it—whether it's iron, citric acid, chocolate, onion soup, or a human being.

"Water is the element of selfless contrast, it passively exists for others....water's existence is thus an existing-for-others.... Its fate is to be something not yet specialized....and therefore it soon came to be called 'the mother of all that is special.'"

—HEGEL, *PHILOSOPHY OF NATURE*

The Magic of Negative Ions

Some say that the energy in moving water releases a mass of negative ions, which are known to be beneficial to physical and emotional healing. As the water breaks up into drops, the positive ions remain with the larger drops and the negative ions fly free with the fine spray. The finer the spray, the more negative ions are produced.[3] Recent studies show that splashing water on superheated rocks also produces negative ions.

The Ancients Name Spiritual Energy

Before the age of materialism, humans thought it was natural to sense the subtle energies of water.[4] They were conscious of the life force that permeated everything—visible or invisible—and associated it with spiritual energy. They gave this life force many names. It is the Huna's *mana* and the Voodoo's *mojo*. It is the *wana'gi* of the Lakota people of North America and *ch'ulel* to the Maya. The Inca call it *sami* and the Aborgine *djang*. Some words like the Asian *chi* and the Hindu *prahna* have become household words. The best our culture has come up with is "vital essence" or "aura," the word used to describe the energy surrounding the human body that reflects the life force. Perhaps the most familiar term is "the force," coined by *Star Wars* creator George Lucas. This describes the energy field that binds everything in the universe.

Although we don't tend to think of ourselves in this way, the molecules in our bodies carry an electrical charge—and like molecules we emit and receive energy. The human energy field is thought to emit a pulsing, wavelike force that extends as far as four feet around our bodies. People throughout the centuries have observed that this "aura" affects and reflects human emotions.

When our energy flows outward and inward at a constant rate, we feel peaceful and content. The electric field is in balance. When we are feeling sad, angry, resentful, anxious, or confused, the field becomes static or turbulent.

Water has a unique transformational power—especially when combined with prayer—to absorb the energy created by emotions. As the solvent of emotions, it can alleviate feelings of negativity, heaviness, and confusion. Water refreshes, calms, and balances.

Water & Prayer

A universal aspect of ritual bathing is the inclusion of prayer, chanting, or medicine songs that open the door to the grace, blessing, and presence of the Divine.

Prayer and water go hand in hand. Many cultures and religions believe that the subtle energies of water can be affected by prayer. When prayers are offered over water, they believe it absorbs the vibratory patterns of the words as well as healing thoughts and intention. Water is an excellent accumulator of prayer—a sort of spiritual energy storage battery. Water infused with prayer can wash away the negative thoughts and emotions that form the root of many physical and emotional ailments, getting in the way of spiritual clarity.

Native American spiritual healers rhythmically chant and shake rattles over water to enhance its healing properties. Maya shamans place their hands above water and repeat their traditional prayers nine times to enrich and consecrate the water in which their patients bathe. They also instruct their emotionally ill patients to pray fervently over a glass of water and then drink it. Catholic priests make water holy by praying and making the sign of the cross over it. Inca priests and priestesses prayed as they immersed their hands in water flowing through the temple. Ayurvedic healers in India use water to capture the vital essence of gemstones and sacred healing plants.

Japanese photographer Masuro Emoto, in his beautiful book, *The Message from Water,* shows the effect of negative and positive thoughts and energies on water. He exposed water to various subtle energies and then froze and photographed the water crystals. Harmful words and thoughts caused unattractive, murky, forbidding swirls that looked much like polluted water. Loving words and prayer created delicate, intricate, lacelike formations.

Larry Dossey, M.D., in his provocative book, *Healing Words,* describes experiments in which prayer positively affected water, red blood cells, seeds, and plants. It also destroyed cancer cells and helped to heal wounds. He eventually came to realize "that not to employ prayer with my patients was the equivalent of deliberately withholding a potent drug or surgical procedure." In her book *Medicine for the Earth,* well-known teacher and shaman Sandra Ingerman reports that she has detoxified polluted water in a spiritual healing ceremony, which included prayer.

"Water is a conduit for intuition. Water amplifies it, whether it is the shower or a great sea. Whenever you are around water it amplifies intuition. The body is the perfect intuitive receptor because it is two-thirds water. Intuition is a fluid movement, a wave movement, and the body is constantly moving in waves."

—JUDITH ORLOFF, M.D.

Plants and Flowers

Water is a medium for the transfer of energy. The power of plants can accumulate in water, which absorbs the chemical essence of plants to render them usable by the human body.

Some peoples, like the Native Americans and the Maya, consider plants to be spirits that could be called upon for help. Many cultures include plants and flowers in the spiritual bathing experience. In South America it is a common practice for traditional healers to administer *"florecidas"* or flower baths to patients for cleansing of the spiritual body.

Scientific research also supports that idea that plants contain vital healing substances. According to recent studies, plants contain numerous chemical compounds called secondary metabolites. These are natural chemicals that the plant does not need to support its own existence and that may evoke a physiological response in humans.[5]

Bach Flower Remedies

Dr. Edward Bach came up with the Bach Flower Remedies in the first half of the twentieth century. He developed a method that involved collecting flowers and placing them on the surface of spring water in a glass bowl, then leaving them in bright sun for three hours. This transfused the water with energy patterns emanating from the flowers. Dr. Bach believed that these energy patterns matched the energy emissions of human emotions. By ingesting the water infused with the flower energy, people could find emotional balance and harmony within and release from negative emotions such as bitterness, fear, and resentment.

The Jews

Living Tradition, Living Waters

Jews have deeply influenced the way the western world perceives its spiritual relationship with water: From the traditions of these ancient Semites sprang forth those of the Christian and Muslim worlds.

Wandering in the parched Sinai Desert for forty years, Jewish nomads were understandably taken with *mayim hayim*—Hebrew for living waters. These waters are flowing, pure, and fresh; the early Jews thought of God as the fountain of living waters. To have abundant water was a sign of God's favor—and to be deprived of it, a sign of God's anger and judgment.

The Jewish *Tanakh* or bible is rich with stories that invoke the power of water. God's first acts of creation were to separate the heavens from the seas and to move aside the waters to form land. Later, the primordial waters returned to wash away human sins, and humanity, through Noah, was given the opportunity to renew itself. It took a journey into the depths of the sea for the prophet Jonah to be purified from his sin of disobedience.

The rituals of *taharah*, the Hebrew word for purification, are designed to draw Jews closer to God. That *taharah* is a pillar of Judaism is clear from the many rituals that exist to help devotees remove impurity.

The best known taharah ritual is that of total immersion—*tevilah*—in the living waters of the *mikvah* that are said to originate in the four rivers that once flowed through Eden when Adam lived in a state of wholeness and oneness with God. The mikvah, Hebrew for "a gathering together," represents the womb from which all humans enter the world, untouched by sin.

"It is a fountain in the gardens, a well of living waters."

—SONG OF SONGS 4:15

17

Opposite: From the Mikvah Project © 2001 Janice Rubin

To return to the state of oneness with God, the Torah requires Jews to immerse themselves in a mikvah after, among other things, childbirth, contact with the dead, returning from war, and the discharge of semen apart from sexual intercourse. Many mikvah rituals revolve around women. Women are to immerse after menstruating and before marriage. Before the Romans destroyed the Second Temple in Jerusalem, men were more frequent visitors. They were commanded to immerse before entering the holy temple—but when the temple was destroyed, this was no longer a necessity. Yet today, men still visit mikva'ot on certain occasions. Men also use the mikvah at other times, such as before the Sabbath or Yom Kippur, the Day of Repentance. A mikvah is required of those converting to Judaism; the convert is considered a new-born child who needs to be cleansed. Immersion also breaks the convert's bonds of biological kinship to non-Jews and joins the convert to the community of Jews.

A Jew can immerse in the natural waters of a spring, lake, river, well, spring, or rainwater-fed pool built according to Jewish law. Traditional rainwater *mikva'ot* (the plural form of mikvah) must be built into the rock or ground, be completely watertight, and contain forty *sa'ahs*—about 185 gallons of living water. The number forty is rich in associations: A person spends forty weeks in utero, the Great Flood lasted forty days, and the Israelites wandered in the desert for forty years.[1]

Generally, a mikvah is composed of two or three pools. Accumulated rainwater is kept in one pool; an adjacent immersion pool is drained and refilled regularly with tap water. The pools share a common wall with an opening at least two inches wide, through which water from one pool flows freely into the other. Through this "kissing" of waters between the pools, the water of the immersion pool becomes an extension of the natural rainwater.[2] Modern mikva'ot look like small swimming pools and often the rainwater is collected in a tank instead of a pool.

Keeping a Woman "Pure"

Many modern Jews and non-Jews alike tend to think of monthly mikvah use as the domain of a married Orthodox woman of childbearing years. This is due to a commandment that has given the mikvah its troublesome reputation among secular Jews. Leviticus 15 and 18—sometimes called the Laws of Family Purity—prohibit a woman from having sex or touching her husband or his belongings during her period and for seven days (called *niddah*) afterward. This means at least 12 days of sexual abstinence each month. After carefully counting the days, the wife goes to the mikvah to be cleansed so that she can once again touch her husband.

One of the wonderful things about Judaism is that it uses spiritual bathing to consecrate human sexuality. Unfortunately, there are many downsides to the strict interpretation of mikvah laws. For example, single and divorced women and those past menopause are not welcome at Orthodox mikva'ot.

Before the Wedding

Many Jewish women traditionally visit the mikvah shortly before the marriage ceremony, marking the transition from single life to married life. In fact, the mikvah was the original bridal "shower." Claudia Rodin, author of *The Book of Jewish Food,* writes of the bridal celebrations in her grandmother's time in Ortakay, then a Jewish suburb of Istanbul. "On the night of a henna, the day before the wedding, the women of a family accompanied the bride to the *banyo* for the mikvah with great pomp and fanfare, carrying luxurious bath accessories, *el bogo de la novya,* which were sent by the groom with an escort of musicians. The bride was submerged seven times into the water, and the ladies ate pastries and sweetmeats while the band played."

The New Mikvah Movement: Taking Back the Waters

Many contemporary Jews are seeking to revive old practices in new ways that will strengthen their individual connection with God and Jewish tradition. Over the last fifteen years, a small but growing group of women have begun to reclaim the living waters, creating what may now be a full-fledged mikvah revival.

This revival has come about as many non-Orthodox Jews have come to regret the loss of ritual in their lives. Women in particular long to acknowledge the waxing and waning of the moon, the tides of the sea, and the monthly cycle that engenders the creation of life and is the basis for the Jewish calendar. Rather than fashion an entirely new ceremony or abandon the mikvah to the Orthodox, they have begun to redesign this 3,000-year-old ritual.[3]

Today, as the practice of religion gradually shifts towards enlightened spiritual renewal, women—and men, too—are rediscovering the beauty of a tevilah and giving the experience new meaning. Spiritual renewal has replaced "uncleanliness" as the focus of the mikvah. New rituals have been created and old ones revisited to mark passages of life; to address a troubling dream or nightmare; to celebrate the new moon and the new year; to pray for fertility or honor the birth of a child; to acknowledge a miscarriage or divorce; to observe holidays; to support mother-daughter bonding; and "just because." Today, a dip in the mikvah helps us to appreciate what came before and to prepare for what is to come. We become more conscious of what we do and who we are, renewing our spiritual integrity.

A Brief History of the Mikvah

The site of many ancient immersions was the longest river in Canaan, the Jordan. The name Jordan means "flowing downward." The river begins at Lake Huleh in the north and flows downward to the Sea of Galilee until it reaches the Dead Sea.

The waters of the Jordan were thought to have a special spiritual and healing quality. In the Old Testament, Naaman, the commander of the Syrian army, received word from the prophet Elijah to bathe seven times in the Jordan in order to be cleansed of his leprosy. The seven immersions cured him, and to this day people still dip in the Jordan River in hopes of being healed.

When Jews settled down and erected cities, they collected rainwater in cisterns for their mikva'ot.

Total immersion was so important that a Jewish community could not be considered a community without a mikvah. Even today, some Jews consider it more central to physical and spiritual life than a synagogue. The bath is often the first religious structure to be built.

Mikva'ot have been unearthed all over the world. Wherever Jews have lived, they have built mikva'ot, even during periods of persecution. Mikva'ot were even hidden under floorboards in homes during the German Third Reich. Thanks to the intricate set of rules governing the building of mikva'ot, these sites have been useful in identifying locations that Jews migrated to and occupied.

WHERE TO GO FOR A MIKVAH

If you'd like to experience a mikvah, call local Reform, Conservative, or Reconstruc-
tionist synagogues and ask for the closest. You can also try Jewish community
centers, adult education centers, seminaries, or universities. Some mikva'ot—such
as Thornhill Community Mikvah in Thornhill, Ontario—offer healing ceremonies.
Mikva'ot run by Orthodox communities or schools may feel intimidating or
uncomfortable to non-Orthodox. Most mikva'ot have limited hours and will not
allow non-Jews to bathe in the water. To make the mikvah more generally
accessible, Anita Diamant, author of *The Red Tent* and nonfiction books about
Jewish ritual, is spearheading an effort to build a pluralistic mikvah, Mayyim
Hayyim, in the Boston area.

Any natural body of water in which you can completely immerse yourself will
serve as a mikvah. It will contain water of divine source and thus, tradition teaches,
the power to purify. Or you can create a non-kosher mikvah in a hot tub or regular
bathtub.

How to Prepare for a Mikvah

The mikvah is not intended for physical cleansing; in fact, before you enter the
mikvah your entire body must be spotlessly clean and free of any loose matter or
foreign objects. The general point is not to let anything come between you and the
water. Note, too, that menstruating women cannot enter the water in most
traditional mikva'ot.

Following are some of the steps to take to prepare for the mikvah before leaving
home:

~ Remove any jewelry

~ Remove your contact lenses

~ Bathe for at least one half hour,
   then shower

~ Shampoo your hair

~ Brush and floss your teeth

~ Wash your face and remove all makeup

~ Remove all nail polish and dirt from
   nails and cuticles

~ Remove all bandages and any adhesive
   residue

~ Comb all hair until free of tangles

~ Use the toilet

Be prepared to shower again before entering the mikvah water.[4]

IMMERSION RITUAL FROM THE TORAH

At most mikva'ot you will find an attendant, called a *shomerit* in Hebrew, to guide you through the steps of the ritual. If no shomerit is available, you may ask a friend to take her place. The custom is to immerse three times. As the shomerit watches, immerse yourself so that every strand of hair is beneath the water and no part of your body is touching the floor or wall, or the surface of the water. After the first immersion, recite the following blessing. It is usually posted on the wall or you can repeat it after the shomerit.

Blessing for Immersion

> *Baruch atah Adonai Elohenu Melech ha olam, asher kideshanu b'mitzvotav vetzianu al ha Tvilah.*

> Blessed Are You Source of Life who sanctifies us with Your Mitzvot and commands us concerning immersion.

Immerse a second time. Upon arising, if you are bathing in a mikvah for the first time or this is a special occasion such as a marriage, say the prayer known as the Shehechiyanu:

> *Baruch atah Adonai Elohenu Melech ha olam, shehechiyanu vekiyyemanu vehiggi'anu lazeman hazeh.*

> Blessed Are You Source of Life, who has kept us alive and sustained us and enabled us to reach this time.

Immerse a third time. After that, you may immerse as many times as you like and add prayers of your own choosing.

"Living waters are purifying waters. The running water of rivers is often used ritually for purification, or where it is not available the pouring of water may accomplish the same aim."

—MIRCEA ELIADE

MIKVAH MEDITATIONS

Each of the following meditations can be done, in turn, before the traditional three immersions in the ritual bath.

Letting Go of the Past (Gently)

Take a deep, slow breath. Feel the water around you. Let it wash and cleanse every part of you…. Let the tender waves of the mikvah carry off your hurts, cleanse your sore spots. Think of things in the past—finished relationships, negative behaviors, violations and losses. Let this womb hold you. Feel its strength and purity. Let it wash away the pain and sadness. Allow yourself a moment of parting from these things. It is time to say goodbye to these parts of your past. Watch them float away. Feel the warm water surround you, comfort you, bathe you. This is the womb of humanity. Let it rebirth you.

Immerse.

Recite the blessing for immersion.

Feeling the Present (Keep It Slow)

Breathe. Feel the sense of your own well-being. Where are you at this moment? Feel your body…. your toes, your legs, your buttocks, your genitals, your belly. Feel the water soothe your back; feel the wetness on your shoulders, your neck, and your face, in your hair. Feel this moment. Feel the life force in your body. Float in the warm liquid, in the sacredness of this event. Feel the mayim hayim (living waters) merge with you. Feel your connection to this place, to this moment, to the Jewish people, to humanity, the universe, and eternity.

Immerse.

Say the following prayer:

> *Shema yisra'el adonai eoloheinu adonai ehad.*
>
> Hear O Israel, Adonai Our god, Adonai is one.

From *Meditations for the Mikvah* by Jane Litman[5]

Welcoming the Future (Slowly, Slowly)

Stretch your body. Breathe. Think of your future. Let the water's spiritual tide bring your desire. What do you want as a person? Feel the water wash you with love, with contentment, with the joy of life, with the presence of God. Imagine all the possibilities that await you. Envision yourself celebrating your new identity. Bathe yourself in the promise of fulfillment that your choices will bring.

Immerse.

Say the Shehechiyanu.

A Jewish Kabbalah Meditation for a Spiritual Bath

Some of the medieval Jewish mystics and authors of the body of writings known as the Kabbalah believed that water reflects our highest and deepest dimensions of self. The human goal should be "to allow the river of light—the deepest current of consciousness—to rise to the surface and animate our lives."[6] It's no wonder that gazing at water became a Kabbalistic technique of meditation and the prophet Ezekiel saw divine visions reflected in the water.

While bathing, keep your thoughts focused on the following:

> At Creation, the light of God filled the void, leaving no room for anything other than God. God withdrew his light and sent one ray into the void, pouring light into vessels. Some vessels couldn't withstand the power of the light and they shattered. While most of the light returned to its divine source, the rest fell as sparks along with shards of the vessels. Eventually the sparks became trapped in material existence. Our human task, say the mystics, is to liberate or to raise these sparks and restore them to divinity. This is the process of *tikkun,* repair or mending, accomplished through living a life of holiness.

Rosh Kodesh Mikvah Ritual

Rosh Kodesh, literally the head of the month, is a new moon holiday for women. Light candles and say this blessing:

> *Baruch atah adonai, m'chadash hachadashim*
>
> Blessed are you, lord, who renews the months

Immerse, then say this blessing:

> May it be your will, Source of life, our God, and the God of our ancestors, that you renew us for this month, for goodness and for blessing. May you give to us long life, a life of peace, a life of goodness, a life of blessing, a life of nourishment and sustenance.

Baby Welcoming Ceremony

Use a roomy portable tub as a mini-mikvah. Fill it with warm water from a good-sized moving source, such as a nearby river or ocean, or use natural or bottled spring water. One or both parents can dip the child in it up to the head or neck.

Recite the blessing for immersion (page 22) before dipping.

When baby is immersed, say:

> May the Creator of all life bless you and keep you.
> May the creator make her face shine upon you and be gracious to you.
> May the creator turn her face to you and give you peace.

Traditional Mikvah Prayer for Fertility

> I pray you, God, lord of all the world, god of Abraham, God of Issac, God of Jacob, God of Sarah, God of Rebecca, God of Rachel, and God of Leah, that you have mercy on me that I may conceive tonight, may the child whom I conceive after this immersion be a sage and a fearer of the name of your holiness, and a keeper of the commandments of your holy Torah. God, Lord of all the worlds, hear my prayer and permit your angel who is in charge of souls to take a pure soul and put it into my body...So may it be your will, Amen, Selah.

Adapted from the Yiddish Seder Mitzvas Hanashim (The Order of Women's Commandments) compiled by Rabbi Benjamin Aaron Solnik, c. 1550–1619.[7]

A New Ceremony: The Yom Kippur Bath

What better time for a reflective, ritual bath?

~ Prepare the ingredients for the bath in the afternoon before dinner and/or services.

~ Collect herbs with kindness—rue, lemon balm, rosemary, or other combinations of herbs work wonderfully well.

~ Simmer herbs in a big pot of water, making the house smell fragrant.

~ Strain (optional).

~ Pour off a cupful for after dinner; drink as a before-sundown tea.

~ After dinner and services, fill a tub with water.

~ Put on sacred music, light incense, and place lighted candles around the bath, as well as a small wooden or clay bowl for dipping.

~ Carry the herb water (which will be no longer hot, just warm) to the tub.

~ Climb into the tub.

~ Use the wooden or clay bowl to pour bowlfuls of herb water over yourself (or have someone else do the pouring), chant your favorite prayers all the while.

~ Soak in the tub for at least 20 minutes.

~ Think about the past year—and what you would like to be forgiven for and how you can make amends.

~ Sing; it's amazing how lovely our voices sound when we sing near and above water in an enclosed space like a bathroom.

A Mikvah Experience

I was in my forties before I ever thought to visit a mikvah. I had never been interested in the ritual because it had always been presented to me as a cleansing for women, as if women were dirty. I had cringed at the thought that physical and metaphysical traces of menstruation, that amazing gift so crucial to human fertility, somehow needed to be washed away. However, as I delved into the subject of spiritual bathing, I had recently learned that this interpretation,

prevalent as it is, was not the only one. I could invest the ritual bath with my own meaning, and so I decided, after having tried the spiritual baths of the Maya, to give the mikvah, that vestige of my family's religious past, a try.

First came the prescribed preparations at home. I followed the list, trimming my nails and removing my jewelry. This was fairly easy, since I don't use much in the way of makeup or artificial adornment. However, my mom had recently treated me to a pedicure and I had randomly chosen a sparkly, creamy, ever-so-happy lavender that I was really enjoying. But the rules said the nail polish had to go.

The mikvah was in the basement of Adas Israel, a progressive conservative synagogue not far from my house in Washington, D.C. I had never known it was there. Mikva'ot aren't publicized; they are part of the fabric of community knowledge, one of those things in life you hear about when you are ready. When I arrived, I was greeted by the "mikvah lady" or shomerit, the feminine version of guardian in Hebrew. A shomerit is the guardian of the mikvah. I like to think of the shomerit—which isn't really a very high position in a synagogue hierarchy (sacrilege!)—as the priestess of the holy waters. The woman guarding my mikvah was so lovely, open, and interested in all thoughts about and aspects of water immersion that she fit my idea of what a priestess of the waters would be like.

She had prepared the bath, following ancient rules of mingling waters. The mikvah waters, she explained, had flowed from the Garden of Eden. This mikvah was a small tiled pool in a small tiled room, perfectly quiet, except for a fan. The room had a peaceful, cut-off-from-the-world, womb-like quality. I showered and checked to make sure I had followed the rules, then scampered naked into the water.

Ahh, the water was lovely...easy to enter into...an enveloping warmth. As soon as I entered I could sense its energy. There was something so freeing about being naked in the water. I am a swimmer, and like everyone else I wear bathing suits, which holds me in, but there I was, breasts floating, water running between my legs, feeling at one with the water. I loved it.

As the shomerit watched, I immersed myself in the center of the pool—every part of me, including my hair—while not touching any wall or the floor or the surface. After the first immersion, I said the Shehechiyanu. I thought of the Shekinah. Since Kabbalistic times, Shekinah has become the feminine personification or aspect of God, the emanation of the divinity that is within us. I think of her as the energy that permeates the world and all within it. I immersed myself three times in the water—the river of light —and in the beauty of Shekinah. Then I silently chanted my own prayers, thoughts, and communications to myself and to the world beyond me. The water brought clarity. I felt filled with love.

The mikvah lady left me alone to my own personal meditation. I immersed myself many times, speaking to God in my mind and heart, asking for blessings. We had an honest, meaningful talk, personal and intimate. I felt soothed, and healed, and in touch with the Divine within.

I think that the mikvah is a perfect place to pray. I love water, and praying in the water feels sacred and right. I would attend services every Friday evening or Saturday morning if we gathered at the water instead of in a synagogue sanctuary. The water provides a powerful place in which to pray together. I feel more at home in the sanctum of the mikvah, in the water, than in a seat in a sanctuary. I don't find it easy to pray in synagogues.

The fan came on and its whir reminded me of the wind over a desert sea. I imagined that I was floating in a desert sea under the moon. The warm wind was my companion and carried my messages to and fro.

I could have stayed submerged all day; I didn't want to part from the water. I had to bring myself back to the day-to-day world with the knowledge that the shomerit had other things to do and so did I—and my car might be getting a parking ticket. I rose from the water feeling refreshed and as fluid as the wind.

That evening, I found myself reluctant to take my regular swim. I didn't want to wash off the sacred water so quickly, and my skin felt soft and lustrous. But it was unbearably hot, so I threw on my suit and leapt into the pool for a different kind of immersion. Still, the magic of the mikvah stayed with me, the sacred water mingling with pool water, my everyday ritual bath.

I left my toenails bare for a few days, as a reminder of the waters of Eden, and in honor of the bond between humans—in our natural state—and God. Then I painted my toenails happy purple once again.

—NDE

A Bath on Yom Kippur Eve

All during the day of Yom Kippur eve I thought longingly of a spiritual bath—in between thinking through my role in my share of the year's conflicts and recalling my moments of less than gracious or honest behavior. And so, as we prepared the holiday evening meal, my dear friend Rosita and I also prepared a holiday evening bath, collecting rue, lemon balm, and rosemary from the garden and setting them to simmer on the stove.

As we settled down to eat, the simmering herbs made the house smell fragrant—the aroma of a savory brisket kept coming to mind. After dinner, I drank some of the herb mixture as a tea—a last drink before my fast—and lit a yellow-orange candle. While the water rushed in to fill the tub, I sat down in the big burgundy armchair in the living room and listened to Leonard Nimoy narrate a radio program on music from the Yom Kippur service. Much of the music was soothing and Nimoy's voice vaguely comforting after years in my life as Mr. Spock.

The bath was filled. The lights were off. Rosita lit copal incense in her *incensario*. I placed three votive candles on the lid of the toilet, creating an altar amid the mundane to add glow to the room. The candles flickered, casting gentle shadows on the white porcelain of the sink.

I relaxed in the hot water as Rosita, with her gentle smile, wordless love, and understanding, brought a wood bowl from the kitchen and poured the herb waters over my head. They streamed down my face like a mask, filling my nostrils. She poured the water down my back and over my breasts and belly.

We said prayers, Rosita singing her favorite Mayan chant in Spanish, which I always love listening to. Then she left me to soak with my own prayers and thoughts in the copal smoke and the candlelight. It amazes me how magical my small bathroom can feel during a spiritual bath, how it transforms into a holy place.

I tried lying down in the water. The water was too hot, so I sat up, picking up the little wooden bowl. All the while the Yom Kippur music played on downstairs, floating up to me. The chant I really enjoyed was the *niddah* chant, la da da da dida de da da da...

I sang to the water in the bowl, letting the water take my breath and swell the sound, which reverberated on the tub and tiles, the sound blending with smoke and water. Over and over again I chanted wordlessly.

Then I sang the Shemah. And then I sang my favorite Shalom Alechim, which I associate with angels and the Shekinah—the feminine presence of God in everyone and everything. I learned the song in Jersualem and it was a gift I brought home from there.

Shalom Alechim transported me, and then I lay down in the water, now cooler, and sang the *niddah* chant. My face near the water, voice low. With the help of the water, I could sing from low, deep, meaningful places within myself that I rarely experience. My sins of the year flew into my heart and mind.

Before I climbed out of the tub, I remembered the role of the water and plants in this ritual, and the energy they bring to life. I recalled the joy of living in the sun. I cupped the herb waters in my hands and let them run through my fingers.

After I said my thank-yous, I climbed out, to towel, to bed, to calm thoughts and reading. We brought the copal, rekindled in the incensario, into my room, lighting candles. And so the evening fell to silence, and the holiday continued on.

—NDE

The Sumerians, Mandaeans, and Egyptians

Ancient River People

The Sumerians: Mingling Sweet and Salty Waters

Although the Jews were the first to record their spiritual bathing traditions, they were not the first Semitic people to practice ritual ablutions and immersions. Their traditions are particularly indebted to other Semitic peoples, such as the Sumerians, who roamed the crossroads of Asia, Europe, and Africa.

Leaving behind their nomadic life on the Arabian and Syrian deserts, the Sumerians settled on the fertile plains surrounding the Tigris and Euphrates rivers, which some historians think is the site of the biblical Garden of Eden. Thousands of years before the birth of Christ, they formed one of humanity's oldest known civilizations. Eventually, conquering Akkadians, ancestors of the Babylonians, and the Assyrians came to share their lands and customs, and even their gods.

The civilizations of Mesopotamia saw water as a means of separating the profane from the sacred. Ritual purification was called *na-ri-gu* or *luh-ha*. High priests performed ablutions of *apsu* or sweet water from the Tigris or Euphrates before carrying out their daily priestly functions. Common people also performed their ablutions and immersions in the rivers, although later a special building, the *bitrimki* or washing house, was constructed next to the priest's house or temple.[1] They cleansed themselves on the new moon in a ritual called *a-tu.*

Opposite: Nefertiti, a 14th B.C. century Egyptian queen, and the Egyptian goddess Isis.

The Sumerians believed that the world was created from Nammu, the sea. Then heaven and earth separated, creating room for two primordial gods: the masculine Apsu and the feminine Tiamet. Apsu represented the sweet water from under the earth that filled the rivers, and Tiamet, the chaos and creativity of the saltwater ocean. From the mingling of sweet and salty waters arose all life, as well as new gods.

As the story goes, Apsu was bent on destroying his descendants, but was vanquished by Enki, the creator god. Enki was sometimes depicted as a goddess and was represented as a half goat, half fish—or half human, half sea being. It's from this that the image of Capricorn later developed. Enki was known as Ea to the Babylonians. Enki-Ea became the god of fresh waters, wisdom, invocations, ritual purification, sorcery, incantation, and craftsmen and artists.

Other water deities in the complex web of Mesopotamian cosmology include Queen Inanna, a water goddess closely associated with vegetation and growing grain. Ishtar, a star goddess, was embodied by the planet Venus, a celestial body associated worldwide with women and water. She ruled the streams and canals, irrigation and agriculture, and was referred to as "the daughter of the ocean stream."

The Mandaeans: Immersing in Yardna

One of the cultures most fervently devoted to spiritual bathing was that of the Mandaeans. Members of this two thousand-year-old Gnostic sect related to both Judaism and Christianity regard John the Baptist as the last prophet. There are less than 100,000 Mandaeans today, mostly in southern Iraq and southwestern Iran. Recently, some have fled to Europe, the U.S., Canada, and Australia to avoid persecution.

As dictated by their Great Book, Mandaean lives are ruled by an elaborate system of repeated immersions in *yardna*—fresh, flowing water. They believe in a preexistent Great Life, a personification of the creative and sustaining force of the universe. The symbol of Great Life is living waters. They immerse to connect to this "life fluid," protect themselves, and gain the promise of everlasting life.[2] Unlike Christianity, Mandaean baptism does not imply initiation.

Every morning before sunrise—at the meeting of dark and light—Mandaeans perform an ablution. Triple river immersion is practiced after menstruation or touching of a dead body, sexual intercourse, and other "impurities." After childbirth the new mother and newborn child were immersed three times before they could reenter society. At marriage the bride and groom were immersed in a ritual hut, or *mandi*, and were given new ceremonial clothes. To ease the crossing to the Otherworld,

Island of Ana in the Euphrates River.

the dying were doused three times from head to foot with river water, clothed in new ceremonial dress, and placed on clean bedding facing the North Star. Funerals include ablutions of attendants and objects. *Masbuta*, purification with water, is performed by a priest and takes place on Sundays after major defilements. Vegetables and fruits should be immersed in the river before they can be eaten. Pots and pans also require immersion and purification.

Ancient Egypt: The Sacred Waters of Nun

The Egyptian creation story opens upon the divine waters of Nun: the watery mass of dark, directionless chaos on which the world rested before it was formed. From Nun and his feminine aspect Naunet arose all primeval land, life, and the family of gods whom the Egyptians worshipped.[3] Depicted as a green or blue frog-headed, bearded man, Nun existed in every body of water, from the Nile River to temple pools—even subsoil water—and was the source of the annual flooding of the Nile.

"There were said to be two rivers called the Nile—one that flowed on earth and one that flowed across the sky in heaven."

Sacred Pools and Lakes

Sacred pools and lakes were built around ancient Egypt's temples to symbolize Nun's primeval waters.[4] These lakes and pools allowed both the *hem netjer* (priests) and the *shemsu* (followers) to attend and perform their religious rites in a state of purity. As part of the coronation ceremonies, kings and queens were ritually bathed with waters from these sacred lakes. Even millennia later, Cleopatra was bathed ritually by her many female attendants. Emulating royalty, the rich built pools in their gardens that symbolized religious concepts. They grew lotus and papyrus in the pools and strewed flowers to add fragrance. The pools were stocked with ornamental fish to attract waterfowl.

Birth was consecrated by water: Newborn children were baptized to purify them of "blemishes acquired in the womb."[5] Water also played a crucial role in the journey to the afterlife. At the entrance to the tomb of Tutankhamen VI (1157–1142 B.C.) there is a mural of the king beside two sacred lakes that lie in the nether world that must be traversed by the spirits of the dead as they travel to the halls of judgment. The dead were also bathed. In fact, archaeologists believe that they may have found the world's oldest paved canal—4,500 years old—next to the Sphinx. They believe it was dug to carry sacred Nile water for the ritual death bathing of Pharaoh Chepren. Chepren's pyramid is the second largest in the complex at Giza.

Gods and the Heavenly River

The Egyptians thought of the Nile as male and the lands it enriched as female.[6] The river itself was often depicted as the god Hapi. Although a male, Hapi has two

full breasts, from which the northern and southern branches of the Nile spring. He also holds two vases that represent the northern and southern Nile. Khnemu (Khnum), the water deity with four rams' heads, represents the four sources of the Nile. Osiris, the dying and rising god, is also identified with the Nile as its level sinks and rises again.

The ancients also identified the goddesses Anuket and Isis with the Nile and the inundation and fertilization of the fields.[7] Centuries later, the worship of Isis spread throughout the Roman Empire competing with Christianity. There was even a temple dedicated to Isis in downtown Pompeii as well as a symbolic Nile. The Pompeii Nile consisted of a double channel, about two acres long, that worshippers flooded to celebrate the annual inundation of the Egyptian river.[8]

Egyptian eighteenth dynasty bas-relief wall painting, ca. 1348-1320 B.C.

Washing the Gods

As human being sometimes bathe before making contact with the sacred, so did the gods sometimes wash before exposure to ordinary people. As part of the highly elaborate morning ritual of the Egyptian temple, statues of gods were purified with incense, water, and natron. Natron, a natural deposit of sodium carbonate that forms as a saline lake evaporates, was also used in mummification.[9]

Post-Partum Bath

After giving birth, Egyptian women were secluded in birth-houses, where they had to purify themselves through ablutions and incense for fourteen days before they could return to their homes.[10]

BATHING & HEALING RITUAL

Sumerian-Style New Moon Bath Ritual

Sumerians knew that the moon phases affect all natural bodies, including water, plants, and especially human emotions. Moon cycle changes are a good time for a ritual of renewal or initiation. The new moon phase is a time of symbolic rebirth. So, when you need to start a new project, welcome a new phase of life, or celebrate a major change for the better, new moon baths are the best.

The new moon comes two weeks after the full moon. The sky is very dark, many stars are visible, and for most of the night no moon is visible—only a silver sliver of a crescent moon appears, first before sunrise, then just after sunset. As the full moon begins to wane, it is time to contemplate what your new moon bath will be about. This helpful meditation will give you focus and purpose. Ask yourself what you would like to accomplish. What do you wish to manifest in this coming transition? When you have the answer, write it down in a clear, concise sentence on a piece of paper and place it on your altar or under your pillow.

When the night sky is completely dark, with no moon or only a slight crescent, it is time to prepare your bath. During the day, choose some plants that grow near you—no matter where you live, there are plants. For this ritual, consider motherwort, plantain, hyssop, St. John's wort, marigold, or basil in any combination or singly. Ideally, plants should be picked with prayers of gratitude and faith stating your purpose and intention.

Sometime that evening or late afternoon, when you have a few hours of undisturbed time, follow the general instructions for flower baths. As you step into the bath, or, if you prefer, before you dip and pour, repeat your intention of renewal, just as you wrote it down, nine times. During the bath, meditate and try to keep your mind focused on this outcome. Give thanks for its fruition as if it were already a reality.

The Christian World

Of Water and the Spirit

At the dawn of the twenty-first century, Christian baptism is one of the world's best-known water initiation rituals. While the mention of such rituals conjures up visions of Christian priests and ministers sprinkling foreheads or dipping the faithful into water, it is by no means original to Christianity. The Sumerian, Babylonian, Assyrian, Jewish, Egyptian, Greek, Roman, Hindu, Maya, and Aztec peoples all found renewal and purification in some sort of similar rite. Even the word baptism has a pre-Christian origin: the Greek word *bapto* or *baptizo,* which means to wash or to immerse.

Early Christians were schismatic Jews who based their spiritual bathing practice on the Old Testament's *tahara* or purification rituals. One ritual in particular struck a chord with Christians. In addition to male circumcision, converts to Judaism were required to immerse in natural water before they could be accepted into the Jewish community. Christianity eliminated the unpopular ritual of circumcision and focused on baptism.

When we began our foray into the world's spiritual bathing traditions, we had no idea how much history was tied up in the sacrament of baptism. As it turns out, the development of baptismal thought and practice plays a major role in the story of Christianity.

"It is by entering the mystery of water that we begin to understand why, in order to save man, we must first immerse him in water."

—ALEXANDER SCHMEMANN,
OF WATER AND THE SPIRIT

39

Opposite: *Baptism of Christ* 1450s, Piero della Francesca, tempera on panel.

John the Baptist

John the Baptist set the course for Christian baptism when he conducted the most famous baptism of all, that of Jesus Christ in the Jordan River. When Jesus was baptized in the cold, flowing waters, two miracles were said to have happened. "And immediately, coming up from the water, he saw the heavens parting and the Spirit descending upon Him like a dove. Then a voice came from heaven, 'You are my beloved Son, in whom I am well pleased.'" [1]

John was a former hermit and recluse who ate locusts and wild honey and wore clothing made of camel's hair with a leather belt around his waist, clothing that was strange even for that time. According to Luke, he appeared in the desert proclaiming a baptism of repentance for the forgiveness of sins. The people of the Judean countryside and all the inhabitants of Jerusalem streamed out to be baptized by John in the Jordan River. [2]

John's message about baptism was different from other contemporary Jewish religious teachings on ritual bathing. He taught the people who came to him that when they repented and confessed their sins during baptism, they would be morally

The Essenes

Some scriptural scholars believe that John the Baptist was a member of the Essenes, a small Jewish sect with around 4,000 members who strictly observed the Sabbath, and believed in the transformational power of water. Essene water rituals influenced the course of Christianity more than those of Jesus' sect, the Nazarenes, a group who practiced ritual bathing more in line with that of other Jewish groups.

The Essenes, authors of the Dead Sea scrolls, settled in Qumran near the Dead Sea around the end of the second century B.C. They practiced a level of ceremonial purity that demanded scrupulous cleanliness. It was obligatory for them to immerse themselves in cold pools before each of their two daily meals. A purifying bath was also required after any contact with the lower classes or strangers. Some devout members bathed as often as five times per day.

The Essenes built 117 ritual bathing pools in Qumran, similar to those discovered at the Temple Mount in Jerusalem. The cisterns were filled by an elaborate water system from an aqueduct in the surrounding hills, a testament to the Essenes' superior engineering skills. The Essene settlement was destroyed when the Romans conquered Qumran and dispersed the sect.

cleansed. Once cleansed, they were ready to accept Jesus. In the scriptures of John the Apostle, Jesus addressed the importance of baptism for the salvation of his followers: "Unless a man be reborn again of water and the Spirit, he cannot enter into the kingdom of God."[3] The Jewish authorities were uncomfortable with John because his baptism symbolized a divine pardon of sins and the advent of a new messianic era that they did not believe in.

St. Paul, originally a Jewish Pharisee known as Saul of Tarsus, took John's ideas one step further. He looked upon baptism as a "watery grave" in which we bury our former, sinful life and proclaim faith in the death, burial, and resurrection of Jesus. It was St. Paul who first connected the neophyte's ritual baptism in water to Christ's death and rebirth to a new and spiritual life. Paul declared that "Sin is not washed away by flowing water, but by the Lord's death and resurrection. Just as Christ was resurrected a spirit, our rising out of the baptismal waters of total immersion enables us to 'walk in a new life.' Buried under the waters of baptism we are raised up to share the power of Christ's resurrection."[4]

Baptism Today: Sprinkle or Immerse? Infant or Adult?

When Christianity first emerged, adult converts who acknowledged Jesus as the messiah were baptized in streams and rivers. The sacrament of baptism was then performed once a year at Easter to symbolize the death and resurrection of Christ. In both ceremonies, converts "died" in their old life and were reborn into Christianity, emerging from the "watery grave" to walk in the "newness of life." There were few variations in how baptism was practiced.

However, as Christianity evolved through the ages, different sects established their own baptismal traditions. By the Middle Ages, most baptisms were conducted inside churches or homes in tubs or pools. Variations began to develop that would splinter the Christian church.

The Christians Decide on Infant Baptism

St. Augustine was the author of the concept of "original sin." As he saw it, each human was born with a stain of original sin on the soul that prevented its entrance into Heaven. He believed that baptism washed away original sin. As a result, the Christian baptism ritual changed significantly: They began to baptize babies between the age of three and four months old instead of as adults. Christians added another new wrinkle to baptism; by the Middle Ages, churches were no longer immersing applicants, but using small baptismal fonts to sprinkle the forehead of infants in an act known as *infusino.*

The Catholic Sacrament of Baptism

Catholic baptisms are performed in church in front of parents, godparents, family, and friends. At this time the child, dressed in white, is also officially named and welcomed into the spiritual community of the church. A priest performs the ritual, saying: "I baptize thee in the name of the Father, Son, and Holy Ghost."

After sprinkling the infant with water, the priest anoints the top of its head with chrism (oil), making the sign of the cross, and says:

> CATHOLIC BAPTISM PRAYER
>
> May Almighty God, the father of Lord Jesus Christ, who has given you a new birth by water and the Holy Spirit who has forgiven of all of your sins, consecrate you with the chrism of salvation in the name of Jesus Christ our Lord unto Eternal life. Amen.

In times of emergency, such as pre-baptismal death, any lay person may baptize another with water by sprinkling it over the forehead and saying the same words.

In recent decades the Roman Catholic Church has made an effort to rediscover ancient church traditions and reform its sacraments. As a result, for the first time in many centuries some Catholics are once again being baptized by being dipped into a pool of water.[5] Some congregations have even built immersion pools in their sanctuaries.

Protestant Adult Baptism—the Anti-Baptists!

Protestant Baptism Prayer

"Let this servant of Christ be baptized in the name of the Father and of the Son and of the Holy Ghost."

When Martin Luther and other Protestant leaders broke with the Catholic church, they returned to some of the precepts of the early Christians. The distinction between baptism at birth and baptism at maturity had been debated by church leaders for centuries, and the Protestants sided with baptism of adults. These dissidents earned the name *Anti-Baptists.*

Supporters of adult baptism point out that there is no mention of infant baptism in the Bible. They believe that baptism should occur when a person repents and accepts Jesus, and that baptism is only meaningful when the person is of an age to consciously make these decisions.

Protestant children were not baptized by immersion; instead, they were sprinkled with water and "christened" as followers of Christ. The Greek word *christos* means anointed one.

Baptists Do It Their Own Way

Baptists first appeared in England and America in the early seventeenth century. They shared many of the beliefs of other Protestant groups, insisting that only adult believers should be baptized. However, unlike some Protestants, they were and are staunch proponents of total immersion rather than the sprinkling or pouring of water in baptismal rites.

Holy Waters: The Eastern Orthodox Day of Epiphany

At no time is the power of water more visible than on January 6, the Day of Epiphany, which in the Byzantine liturgical calendar is the day of Jesus' baptism. On this day, priests bless the waters, and churchgoers bring empty bottles to fill with the blessed water. They use the water to sprinkle their houses and venerate icons by immersing their fingers in the blessed water, then touching the icon. Later the priests themselves go to houses and bless them with holy water, beginning the annual season of house blessing.

On this day, the wedding Feast of Cana (and, symbolically, the marriage between Christ and the church) is also celebrated. This was the wedding at which Jesus turned water into wine, much as Moses turned the Nile river water into blood to convince his people that it was his mission to liberate them. Just as the water was changed, so the world is called upon to transform itself on the Day of Epiphany.[6]

The Baptism, ca. 1400–1450, courtesy of The State Russian Museum.

Holy Water

"Whoever believes in me, let him drink....streams of living water shall flow out from within him."

—JESUS, GOSPEL OF JOHN, NEW TESTAMENT

Holy water is water that has been consecrated by priestly blessing for symbolic use in ritual sprinkling or immersion. It is said to absorb, store, and transmit the prayerful intention of the priest. It has been used in the purification rites of ancient Greek, Roman, Egyptian, and Jewish religions as well as in the Latin and Eastern Christian churches.[7] Ancient Jews created holy water by mixing the ashes of a sacrificial red heifer with water. Whatever the religion, the ceremonial use of holy water signifies spiritual cleansing. It is also used to invoke the gods' protection and, in conjunction with prayer, to expel evil spirits.

Roman Catholics use three different kinds of holy water. Baptismal water is consecrated with holy oils at Easter. Churches, altars, and altar stones are consecrated with water in which wine, salt, and ashes are mingled. Specially prepared Easter water is used to bless homes at Easter.[8] To prepare Easter water, the priest plunges a candle into water, signifying the sanctifying descent of Christ into the waters of the Jordan. He then pours in chrism—a combination of olive oil and balm consecrated on Holy Thursday—in the form of a cross, to signify that the Spirit, symbolized by the oil, makes the water an instrument of holiness.

Even today, Catholics upon entering a church follow the ancient custom of dipping their fingers into a bowl of holy water and making the sign of the cross over their head and chest. At certain Catholic ceremonies, the priest walks through the aisles sprinkling holy water on the faithful as a symbol of purification and renewal in Christ.

Catholic mystics tell tales of using holy water to scare away evil spirits who slipped into their meditations with Christ. One such mystic was St. Teresa of Avila, a sixteenth-century Carmelite nun who for many decades of her cloistered life experienced wonderful and awful visions of heavenly and satanic beings. She declared that when the other sisters doused her with holy water, the evil spirits fled like a crowd of people leaving a burning building.

SPIRITUAL BATHING RITUALS

How to Use Holy Water from the Church in Your Home

Most Catholic churches make holy water easily available to parishioners from basisns called fonts, which are often found close to the entrance of the church. If yours doesn't have one, ask the priest how to get some. Holy water is usually used in conjunction with the words, "In the name of the Father, the Son, and the Holy Spirit."

There are many possible uses for holy water. Keep a bowl at the entrance to your house and each time you enter, make the sign of the cross over your head and chest. Keep a bowl of it near your bedside to use for the sign of the cross as you awaken or go to sleep. When feeling out of sorts emotionally, dip your fingers into the holy water and make the sign of the cross over each of your palms and your forehead. Babies can be blessed at home in this way, too.

Homemade Holy Water Ritual

Fill a glass jar or vessel with tap or spring water in the early morning hours; sunrise is best. Sit with the jar of water in front of you and hold your hands in or above the water, saying prayers appropriate to your faith.

Place the vessel of water in the light of the rising sun, in a window, on the porch, or in any other safe place where it will be exposed to the sun for most of the day and be left undisturbed by children, neighbors, and pets.

In the evening, use the water in one of two ways. You can pour the contents into a plain, unscented bath and soak for twenty minutes. If you prefer to shower, pour cupfuls over your entire body. While bathing in the sun-soaked water, think about renewal, refreshment, and spiritual enhancement.

Cleanse your energies from the tub by rinsing it with salt water or wiping a half of a lemon over it to freshen up the vibes for the next bather.

Instant Holy Water Bath

Pour out a gallon of fresh, cool tap or spring water. Hold your hands over the container of water and pray for your desired result for five minutes. Take the water into the shower and use an unbreakable dipper to pour it over your body. Be sure to splash the water on your face, over your head, and all around your body. The more splashing and sprinkling you do, the stronger the effect of this bath.

Essential Oil Holy Water Shower

Soak a piece of muslin or cheesecloth in three ounces of water to which you have added one or two drops of your favorite essential oil. Bathe with soap and water as usual, then tie this cloth around the showerhead and let the water flow over you. Meditate on the cleansing and rebalancing of your energies and emotional poise for five minutes. Some good essential oils to use for this purpose are lavender, rose, clary sage, basil, neroli, ylang-ylang, and thyme.

Holy Floral Water

Choose a certain type of flower—such as red roses for love and passion, white roses for spiritual enhancement and overcoming a relationship breakup, or marigold for general spiritual cleansing. Choose one type only; usually one of them will call to you.

Gather the flowers on a bright, cloudless day. While focusing on your intention, pick the flowers, holding a leaf between thumb and forefinger so as not to touch the flower with your fingers. Always give thanks to the plants and their flowers for your healing.

You'll need a clear glass bowl with no etches or designs that can hold up to two quarts of tap or spring water. Still holding each flower by the leaf, drop them into the bowl one at a time until the surface of the water is covered, but not so much that the flowers crowd each other. Set the bowl in the sun for three hours. Strain the water through a cotton cloth.

Bathe by pouring the flower water over your body all at once, or drink it, a few ounces at a time. If you want to use it as an elixir, you can store in the refrigerator for up to two weeks. Add an ounce of rum, brandy, or vodka to preserve the elixir and prevent spoiling for a longer period of time. This florecida can be enhanced by adding crystals or other gemstones to the bowl. If possible, store in containers of colored glass. You can add four drops of the elixir to other liquids or nine drops to your bath water.

Holy Floral Water for the Dinner Table

Try this for a change:

Fill the drinking-water jar for the table and add three roses, three marigolds, a few sprigs of lavender, or a handful of orange blossoms. For spicier water, use three six-inch sprigs of sage, thyme, oregano, or basil. Float them in the water an hour or so before dinner. Your guests will love it.

Life-Change Ritual at the Sea

The ancient practice of thalassotherapy, or bathing in sea water, is an excellent purification ritual. Sea water and its spray are charged with negative ions and magnetically charged elements that balance our emotions.

This is much like the ancients' practice of dipping seven times in the Jordan River for spiritual renewal. It is a good ritual to perform when you are experiencing a difficult time letting go of something from the past, making a rough transition, or just having a hard time dealing with changes in your life.

With a bathing suit underneath, dress yourself in old clothes you're ready to discard—especially one or more items representing something from your "old" life—and go to the sea. Dip your body into the sea seven times, saying with each dip,

"I now break all links with _____ [appropriate phrase]"

Strip off the old clothes and throw them away in a trash bin at the beach. Walk away and don't look back.

Letting-Go Ritual

While contemplating the change you wish to realize in your life, collect nine white flowers of any kind in a basket. Express your thanks to the flowers for their assistance with this ritual.

At noon, go to a fresh, flowing body of water. Standing at the shore, toss the flowers, one by one, into the current, assigning to each one a quality of your pain, sadness, or whatever it is you are now willing to let go of. As each flower hits the water, watch it float away and say: "Good-bye to_____."

This ritual may be repeated if necessary, but usually once is sufficient for renewal and acceptance of change.

Aqua Vitae (Living Water) Bath Ritual

To refresh yourself when life gets overwhelming and over-scheduled, go to an eastern-facing stretch of ocean shore at dawn. Facing the rising sun, sit at the water's edge, allowing the waves to flow over you but not knock you down.

Each time a wave washes over you, say or think to yourself:

"The sea wave is now carrying away my exhaustion and frustration and leaving me renewed."

After several minutes, walk into the sea, face the rising sun, and take a dip, bidding farewell to the old feelings.

Repeat this often, especially if you live by the sea. On a western-facing coastline, you can perform this ritual at sunset.

Ready for Renewal Ritual

Go to a fresh, flowing body of water at noon, taking along a container for water and a bowl. Fill the container with water. With your back to the river or stream, fill a bowl with water from the container and throw the water over your left shoulder nine times.

Each time you toss a bowlful of water over your shoulder, say:

"Goodbye to_____."

You may also think this silently.

The Healing Waters of Lourdes

The sacred spring at Lourdes in France is one of the world's most famous Catholic shrines. It was here, in 1858, that Bernadette Soubirous saw eighteen apparitions believed to be the Blessed Virgin Mary.

Bernadette, a sickly peasant girl of fourteen, was out with two friends gathering wood near a grotto when she first beheld the vision of a lady surrounded by a shimmering golden aura above a rose bush. Frightened by the vision, she fell to her knees to say the rosary. None of her companions could see the vision. Later, at home, when she told of what she had seen, her mother beat her and a villager slapped her in the street "for putting on comedies."

Bernadette and six other girls returned to the grotto the following Sunday. The lady, whom she called *aquero*—dialect for "that one"—appeared again. Bernadette sprinkled holy water over the vision and the lady smiled. Bernadette heard her say, "Would you have the goodness to come here for fifteen days? I do not promise to make you happy in this world, but in the next." Gradually the audience in the old field grew to over eight thousand people—much to the chagrin of the local church authorities, who refused to accept that these were true spiritual visions.

Each time Bernadette asked the lady to identify herself, she only smiled, until on the sixteenth visit she said, "I am the Immaculate Conception." Guided by the apparition, Bernadette discovered a spring in the grotto where people were cured by drinking or bathing. The lady in the vision instructed Bernadette to tell the priests that people were to be allowed to go there and that a chapel should be built on the site of the spring.

One of the first recorded cures was of the two-year-old son of Emperor Napoleon III. The child suffered from serious sunstroke, thought to be complicated by meningitis. The boy's nanny traveled over ninety miles with the ailing infant and secured a bottle of water from the spring. She sprinkled the child and he recovered almost immediately. After this, the emperor ordered the police barricades to be removed and the ritual of devotion began.

Bernadette of Lourdes died in a convent in Nevers, France at the age of thirty-five. Today, Lourdes is a pilgrimage site visited by more than five million people each year. Some are curious; others come in search of miracles and comfort. Since 1858, more than seventy miraculous cures have been officially recorded by the Medical Bureau at Lourdes. Most pilgrims say that they feel more reconciled with their lives and their illness after partaking of the waters at Lourdes.

The Ancient Romans and Greeks

A Healthy Mind, Body, and Spirit

It is not easy for those of us who live in this century to appreciate the heights to which the ancient Greeks elevated bathing. We know that they were pioneers in art, sculpture, literature, science, medicine, and government, but few are aware of one of their most influential innovations: the public bathhouse. Greek public baths were as ubiquitous as movie theatres or gas stations are today, and they were greatly admired by other peoples—in particular, the Romans.

"The Greek ideal of culture was the ideal of health."

—WERNER JAEGER[3]

To the Greeks, bathing was far more than a private, hygienic necessity; it was a way to maintain physical, emotional, and spiritual well-being.[1] Ancient Greek doctors regularly prescribed exercise, healthy diets, intellectual stimulation, and hot baths. The Greek ideal was "a sound mind in a sound body." Plato considered health, beauty, and strength the three physical virtues that had to be balanced by the virtues of the soul—piety, courage, temperance, and justice. Together, these formed the Greek ideal of unity and harmony of body, mind, and soul and the fundamental concept behind the gymnasium. The bath was the heart of the gymnasium complex, and was surrounded by lecture halls and private areas where philosophers such as Plato and Socrates discoursed with their students.

"The way in which a civilization integrates bathing into its daily life, as well as the type of bathing it prefers, yields an insight into the inner nature of that period..."[2]

51

Opposite: Statue of Venus and Baths of Venus at Park of Caserta Palace, Italy.

The larger public baths contained a variety of rooms. The *apodyterium* (dressing area) had niches for clothing and shoes. The *unctuarium* was a room devoted to massage with scented oils stored in large clay pots. The *palaestra,* a central open-air courtyard for exercise, was surrounded by a shady portico that led to the bathing rooms. In the palaestra bathers lifted weights, wrestled, ran, or played ball; some Roman baths, such as the one in Herculaneum, featured a *piscina* or swimming pool. Bathers, accompanied by their slaves, soaked in the *tepidarium* in a pool of warm water or in the *caldarium's* waist-high pool of hot water. The caldarium also had a cold water fountain or labrum for splashing the face and neck.

After the caldarium, the bather might return to the tepidarium before finishing with a refreshing dip in the cold pool of the *frigidarium* or cold room. Another stop was the *laconium,* a hot dry sand bath named after the southern coastal people of Laconica.

The Greek Gods and Water Mythology

Although a deeply religious polytheistic people, the ancient Greeks had no prophets, messiahs, clergy, church, or sacred books that declared a fixed truth or dogma. Its apostles were mothers, elders, and poets such as Hesiod, who recounted their own versions of the legends of gods and goddesses.

Oceanus—The Creation Myth

The Titan Oceanus was the son of Uranus (the heaven) and Gaea (the earth) and symbolized the great stream that girdled the earth. He was a water-serpent deity who surrounded the earth with his vast body, holding his tail in his mouth to form a continuous barrier of water at the outer limits of the world. Oceanus and his sister/consort Tethys (also known as Doris) ruled over the liquid element of the primordial world.[4]

Poseidon

When Zeus overthrew the Titans, Poseidon succeeded Oceanus as ruler of the waters. Originally a god of springs and a freshwater deity, Poseidon gradually evolved into an awesome marine god associated with the wind and the tempestuous forces of water. The Roman name for Poseidon is Neptune, which means to flood. We are all familiar with the image of a bearded and forceful Neptune brandishing his trident to command the storms. He is often shown riding the waves in his chariot pulled by horses, escorted by numerous sea nymphs and mermaids.

The Nereids

Oceanus and Tethys gave birth to countless female nymphs known as Nereids, playful and benign water creatures later called "she-devils" by Christians. Poseidon was said to have fallen in love with the Nereid Amphitrite and to have courted her favors while riding on a dolphin. When Poseidon finally won the heart of Amphitrite, he made her his wife and queen and honored their good fortune by placing the dolphin among the stars.[5]

Achilles

The Greek hero Achilles, who is often associated with water, was the son of the Nereid Thetis and a mortal, King Peleus. Wishing to bestow the immortality of the gods on her son, Thetis dipped Achilles into the River Styx, but neglected to dip the heel by which she held him, so he remained mortal and vulnerable to death.

The River Styx

The River Styx was the river that separated Hades, the Underworld, from the living world. The souls of the dead were ferried from the land of the living by Charon. This belief persisted up to the eighteenth century in countries such as Greece and Ireland. Even though they had converted to Christianity, peasants of these lands still placed a coin in the mouth of the deceased to pay the ferry toll to Charon at the River Styx.

Aphrodite

The great beauty and seductress, Aphrodite, goddess of love and beauty, was also the protectress of sailors; it was she who received the souls of those put to sea in funeral boats. The name Aphrodite, "born of the foam," has this origin: Her father, Uranus, oppressed and mistreated his wife Gaea, until at last Gaea convinced her son Chronos to battle his father. During the struggle, he severed Uranus's penis; the sperm flew over the waves and became the foam that gave birth to Aphrodite.[6]

Aphrodite was the ancestral mother of the Romans because she gave birth to their founding father, Aeneas. Known as Venus to the Romans, she was the mother of Venitti, whose capital city became Venice—the city known as "the queen of the sea" and named after the goddess herself. Aphrodite/Venus was later linked with Cupid or Eros, the bisexual god of erotic love who shot the proverbial arrow of romantic love into the hearts of would-be lovers.

Epidaurus

On the southwest coast of ancient Greece on the Saronic Gulf was a town called Epidaurus. The temple at Epidaurus was the central site of ritual bathing in Greece. Visitors in search of healing could enter a special room in which they would receive a dream vision from the god, explaining the cause of their sickness and its cure. But before they could receive this divine gift, they had to undertake a series of preliminary purifications—known as *katharsis*—that included purging, special diets, and ceremonial bathing by attendants. Sacred snakes were let loose during the night; it was believed that they caused the prophetic and explanatory dream visions, and some illnesses were treated by having the patient licked by snakes.

Relief sculpture of Aphrodite sitting on a seashell. Found in the ancient Greco-Roman city of Aphrodisias.

Through the ages Aphrodite was given fresh names by different cultures: Moira, Marina, Pelagia, and Stella Maris are all titles related to her control of the sea. The Egyptians knew Aphrodite as Mari, the sea, and her island was Ay-Mari.

Most people don't think of Sandro Botticelli's magnificent *The Birth of Venus* as a representation of spiritual bathing—but it is! It is worth a pilgrimage to Florence's Uffizi museum just to visit with the young maiden as she arises naked from the sea on a scallop shell. She represents pure beauty, love, and femininity, and she is forever linked to sensuality, sea foam, and lovemaking.

The Romans: A Civic Bath

The Romans conquered the Greeks, but when it comes to culture, the conquered vanquished the conquerors. The Romans absorbed Greek culture, philosophy, medicine, science, arts, and literature. Enchanted by the Greek public bath, they fashioned it to their own taste, style, and politics. Since going to the bath and maintaining physical stamina and health was a civic and spiritual duty, the *thermae,* as they called their baths, became an integral part of Roman life. Not to bathe daily would have been un-Roman. At one time there were more than a thousand thermae in the city of Rome.

As many as three thousand people could fit into a large Roman public bathhouse at one time. Generally, men set aside the morning hours for business and public affairs and spent the afternoons at the baths, relaxing in the tepidarium and caldarium, enjoying exercise, games, massage, and intellectual pursuits. Respectable women bathed in the morning, apart from the men. In the evening hours, the bathhouses became the site of revelry and festive occasions. Because the public baths were outside the jurisdiction of local authorities, they often swarmed with prostitutes.[7]

It was in the bathhouse that Romans sought and found congenial companionship and simple pleasures, in an atmosphere that allowed no room for distinction between classes. Centurions bathed and conversed with commoners, and all could gain the advantage of intellectual discourse and discussion. Bathhouses were major cultural centers that helped to integrate the individual into the mainstream of the nation. The best artwork of the day was displayed and there were performances of theater and music, as well as sporting events.[8]

Roman leaders and wealthy merchants considered the care and keeping of the baths a top priority. Records of official expenditures of government taxes show that as much as one third of public funds went toward the building and meticulous maintenance of public baths.

The Romans carried their bathing tradition to all the lands that they conquered. After having vanquished and sometimes destroyed an enemy city, the Romans wisely ceded a major portion of the reconstruction budget to lay out the bath-gymnasium, which often went a long way toward political pacification.

Ancient Baths and Buildings

Hundreds of artisans and craftsmen toiled together to create ornate, classical bathhouses, funded by the state or a wealthy patron. Inside, statues and shrines were erected for the worship of the Imperial Cult, reflecting the might and munificence of the empire. Some of the better-preserved Roman baths are the Imperial Thermae in Trier, Germany, and the Thermae of Diocletian in Rome. Built around A.D. 300, the Diocletian is located in a densely populated area between two of Rome's seven hills; it has recently been renovated and opened to the public. In the Swiss city of Zurich there is also an impressive display of an excavated Roman bath.

Baths of such magnitude required massive amounts of water. To supply them, engineers built extensive aqueduct systems that carried water over tiers and arches to the cities and towns. Rome's eleven aqueducts carried in ninety million gallons of fresh water each day. This water was sent to public fountains for drinking, to the thermae for baths, and to homes and public buildings.

Many bathhouses were built over natural hot springs that heated the bathing rooms from below. When such springs were not available, the baths were heated with braziers or through heat ducts under the floor. Special thick-soled sandals were needed to protect feet from the heated floors.

A room in a thermae, Herculaneum, Italy.

Roman Water Gods

The Romans didn't worship gods or goddesses before they were exposed to the Greeks. Although many prominent Romans scorned the Greek gods, a Roman Pantheon began to become popular around 550 B.C.. The Zeus-like Jupiter, god of heaven and thunder, was the protector of Rome and the guardian of the faith; Poseidon was renamed Neptune. The twelve deities were divided into six divine couples: Jupiter and Juno, Neptune and Minerva, Mars and Venus, Apollo and Diana, Vulcan and Vesta, and Mercury and Ceres.

Diana and Egeria

Diana was the mistress of the rivers. Like her Greek counterpart, Artemis, she haunted pools and waterfalls as well as grottoes, which mortals were forbidden to enter. Her main abode was at the sacred grove of Nemi. Later, Christians saw her as a major rival and ordered the destruction of her temples. Many of these temples were converted into churches, then honored as the site of various legends in the life of Mary.

Egeria, a water nymph, lived in the grove at Nemi with Diana. Her lover was the king Numa Pompilius. The marriage of Numa and Egeria, celebrated every May in the sacred grove, was symbolic of the sacred union between the powers of vegetation and water that occurred each spring to renew the fertility of the earth. Egeria was also associated with healing. The spring of Egeria gushed forth from a great oak tree whose water was said to confer prophetic visions. Many still believe this spring is endowed with miraculous attributes.[9]

Roman Nereids

The Nereids, who attended Diana as her handmaidens, were divided by the Romans into two types: Spring and river nymphs brought nourishment to the earth; sea nymphs protected sailors from shipwreck. They were all honored with prayer and sacrifice—and they were known to mingle amorously with mortals.[10]

In their public baths, the Romans and Greeks created a perfect medium for bridging the gap between body and mind, one that was within the reach of the ordinary people. The rise of Christianity, however, spelled the end of the public bath in most of Europe. How wonderful it would be to regain this breadth of state-supported cultural and recreational activities and once again elevate the public bath to the heights it deserves.

Rain Charms for the New Year

The Romans, Greeks, Macedonians, and Assyrians used rain-charms that involved sprinkling water on the ground with prayers, incantations, and rituals to bring on the rain.[11] Even today, as a New Year's purification rite some peoples sprinkle water on each other and on implements and buildings. The Tarahumara Indians of northern Mexico sprinkle their ploughs with water as a rain charm; in India, oxen are sprinkled with water before the first plowing of the season.

The Muslims

Bathing for Allah

In the seventh century, the angel Gabriel recited the Koran to his messenger Muhammad, the man whom Muslims consider to be the last in a line of prophets that includes Abraham, Moses, and Jesus. Born in the arid lands near Mecca, Muhammad and his followers highly valued water and the state of ritual purity. Muhammad was impressed with the purification rites of neighboring Middle Eastern peoples, especially the Jews, and borrowed heavily from their written traditions.[2] Today, the rituals Muhammad recommended are practiced by one-fifth of the world's population—even those who live in verdant tropical lands.

> *"The key to Paradise is worship: the key to worship is purification."*
>
> —MUHAMMAD[1]

Taharah

Before entering the mosque, Muslims are required by the Koran to perform *tahara*—the ritual cleansing and purification of the body and spirit that prepares devotees for communion with Allah. There are fountains and pools of pure rainwater outside of mosques for this purpose.

Muslims believe that tahara restores worshippers to a state of purity before they enter the mosque. Prayer is thought to be more heartfelt, and guidance from Allah to come more readily to those who have been purified.

Wudu, Ghusl, and Tayammum

Wudu is a ritual partial washing of the body that removes impurities arising from urinating, breaking wind, touching a dog, minor bleeding from wounds, the loss of consciousness, or an interval of sleep. Before prayer, the personal practice of Muhammad is to: wash the mouth, the throat, and the nose; bathe the whole face in water; bathe both hands and arms to the elbows; rub the head with water; bathe the feet to the ankles.

The most important Muslim ablution is *ghusl,* a ritual washing of the whole body that removes impurities resulting from sexual intercourse, ejaculation with or without coitus, menstruation, childbirth, major bloodletting from wounds, or contact with a corpse. *Ghusl* is also part of the preparation for conversion to Islam and a pilgrimage to Mecca.

The third type of ritual ablution is *tayammum.* When water is not available for bathing or can't be used, devotees can clean themselves with sand, earth, or unfashioned stone.[3]

The Hammam

"Your town is only a perfect town when there is a bath in it."

—ABU SIR

Around A.D. 600, Muhammad recommended sweat baths to enhance the fertility of his followers and help them to multiply. Until that time, the Arabs had bathed only in cold running water. But when the Arabs conquered Syria, they were captivated by Greek and Roman bathing customs. Adopting the practice, they named their sweat bath the *hammam,* Arabic for "spreader of warmth."[4]

It is said that in A.D. 642, when the Arabs defeated the Egyptians in Alexandria, they heated the city's Roman baths for six months with papyri from the renowned Ptolemaic Library. It is believed that they burned as many as 700,000 works to satisfy their newfound fascination with hot baths. Later, as they conquered the rest of Northern Africa and Spain, they converted some Jewish temples and Christian churches into hammams.

The oldest known hammams are those of the semi-Bedouin Camayyad caliphs. The caliphs preferred the freedom of the desert to the constraints of town life, so they built their hammams outside of cities. The Kusair'Aman, one of the oldest hammams in the Middle East, stands alone on a barren plain near the Dead Sea.

The Hammam and Spiritual Life

The Arab public baths gradually took on religious significance. To make it easier for Muslims to comply with Islamic laws of hygiene and purification, hammams were annexed to mosques, and worshipers were particularly encouraged to visit the hammam before evening prayers. It also became popular to visit the hammam to celebrate rites of passage. It was customary to bathe before donning new clothes, and after making a journey, recovering from an illness, attending a funeral, or being released from prison. Eventually, the hammam became known as "the silent doctor" for its purported power to cure ailments such as rheumatism, skin ailments, and infertility.

A Woman's Gathering

At first women were forbidden to enter the hammam, but once its health benefits were realized, women were allowed in after an illness or childbirth. Eventually, they were allowed to go daily if they wished, to enjoy each other's company, gossip, henna their hair, and sing together. The hammam became such an important part of daily life for a Muslim woman that a woman had grounds for divorce if her husband forbade her to go to the bath.

In all Muslims countries, the most important preliminaries to the wedding rite are purifying the bride with water and painting her with henna. The bridal bath takes place a day or two before the ceremony and the bride's departure for the groom's house. During the bath, the mother of a groom can get a close-up look at her prospective daughter-in-law to ensure that she has no deformities and appears, at least outwardly, healthy and fit for childbearing.

Hammams Today

During the late nineteenth century the hammams entered a period of decline. They were stripped of their fine carpets, ornaments, and mosaics and allowed to lapse into decay. The ones that still exist today are often mere shadows of their former selves. Lovely ones can be found in the homes and villas of prosperous Muslims. Where they do exist, in old Arab cities like Istanbul, they still offer bathers a wonderful experience.

In the nineteenth century in Europe, everything Oriental was in fashion and "Turkish baths" took their turn on the social scene. The custom spread to Germany, England, and Australia, then finally to America—where it was not embraced with equal enthusiasm. In America, the Industrial Revolution left little time for such pleasures in the lives of the workers, unless they were immigrants from the Middle

East who viewed the bath as a necessity, not a luxury. Turkish baths still go in and out of vogue; they can be found in cities around the world.

A visit to the bath traditionally required much preparation. Women brought along soap, henna, towels, stools, and rugs—and their children. The elegance and extravagance of the early hammam for women is depicted in books and paintings on Arab life. Women sit unveiled, gossiping, laughing, suckling their children or painting their faces, leaving their hair in top-knots while the henna soaks in. Servants and attendants bring in platters of fresh fruit, fans, and switches for beating the body. Women and children converse as they lie languidly on couches and magnificent handwoven rugs, while shafts of light mix with steam to create a mysterious fog in the confines of this very feminine place.

The Harem by Achille Boschi, (1852–1930). Oil on canvas, 22 x 32 inches, reproduced courtesy of Mathaf Gallery, London.

A SPIRITUAL BATHING RITUAL

The Home Hammam for Friends or Couples

Many generations have found the hammam to be a fulfilling spiritual and soothing experience. To create a mini-hammam at home, you just need a few items: Bring an oriental carpet into your bathroom. Fill the tub with hot water and close the doors and windows to allow the steam to build up in the room. Put on Turkish, North African, Sephardic, Sufi, Islamic, or world music or chants. Light a few candles. Say an opening prayer to rid the bathroom of jin, evil, or troublesome spirits. Climb into the tub, and wash each other's hair, backs, and arms. Talk, pray, relax. While waiting for your hair to dry, massage each other vigorously with a dry washcloth or loofah. Finish off with a cup of mint tea or Turkish coffee.

A Turkish Bath:
A Young Tourist Experience

When I was a teenager in the late 1970s, I wandered—by myself, as was my wont in those days—through Istanbul, full of curiosity about Byzantium and the city where east and west meet. I visited the Topkapi Palace, the Sancta Sophia, and the Blue Mosque and had a breathless escape (chased by men) after stumbling into a red-light district where women were on display in cages. I smoked tobacco in a four-foot water pipe and drank thick coffee and argued politics with young Turkish men who fancied themselves radicals.

Also on my youthful tourist wish list was a visit to a Turkish bath. I really didn't know what a Turkish bath was; I just knew that I wanted to experience one while I was in Istanbul. I had no idea what to expect, but I imagined it would be soothing.

I asked at the youth hostel about the location of a bath, then wound my way through narrow streets to the Cagaloglu Hamami or old Turkish Bath near Sancta Sophia and the Yerebatan Caddesi, an underground cistern built by Byzantine Emperor Justinius in the sixteenth century.

It was winter, and cold, and the bath was in a cavernous old building that looked straight out of Moorish Byzantium. It was built by Cigale Sinan Pasa in the sixteenth century, then restored and reopened by Sultan Mahmut I in the eighteenth century. At the time of my visit the building wasn't too well heated, and although it once may have been painted brightly, I remember the building as feeling and looking rather drab.

I paid a small fee and was sent through a hallway into the dimly lit ladies' bath. A vaulted ceiling stretched over the steamy main pool; around it the floor was tiled. It was midday and there were not many women there.

Upon entering I was assigned to a bath attendant. I hadn't really realized that any attendants were involved in the bath and I was a little uneasy. She was short and squat and naked from the waist up, with rolls of fat cascading down her belly. Her arms were thick; her hands, powerful. She didn't seem to smile (*Ahh, yet another young hapless American tourist,* she must have been thinking) and she didn't speak a word of English. I think she tried to communicate with me but I was too nervous to respond. She grunted and handed me a towel, sending me scurrying into one of many small dressing rooms to remove my clothes.

I had never been to a public bath before—it simply wasn't part of the experience of growing up in American suburbia—and although I was anxious to experience the world, the idea of taking off my clothes and getting into a pool with people I didn't know made me uncomfortable. Naked, with the skimpy towel around me, I was herded into the steamy water. I enjoyed the water and wondered about the traditional bathing ceremony advertised in the brochure. None of the other patrons paid any attention to me while I was in the water.

When I came out of the bath, I was handed over to my attendant. She gestured for me to lie down on a towel on the floor. I did and she vigorously rubbed and scrubbed my skin. At age eighteen I had never had a massage before, and I was shocked by vigor of this one. I tried to stay calm while the woman walked on my back. I am sure I must have looked terrified, because I was. As soon as she let go of me, I raced to my cubby.

She brought me tea and a dry towel. Sipping the tea, I used the time to reflect and cool down. Eventually I roused myself, dressed, and went back out into the streets of Istanbul, another experience chalked up for my trusty old journal.

—NDE

The Hammama Mammas

My Iranian grandparents often regaled us with tales of the old country that made it all seem like an exotic paradise. While traveling in Morocco in 2001 with a group of female physicians to observe women's and children's health-care programs in that country, I had the chance to fulfill a long-held wish to visit a hammam in the Muslim world. For years I had nursed fantasies of lavishly appointed rooms with arabesque arches, tiled walls and floors, and perfumed air—a dimly lit, curtained, harem-like environment for women only—where I would receive exotic skin treatments and luxuriate in hot baths, attended by veiled women, while exotic Arabic music played in the background.

The Morocco itinerary did not include a visit to a hammam, but when our delightful guide told us that she frequented one regularly in her neighborhood, I begged to be taken there when we were passing through her home city. Our group was made up of Americans, none of whom had ever been to an Islamic public bath, and of course every other woman on the trip wanted to come along. So, late one night, after a full day of hot and dusty driving through the arid Atlas Mountains, Amina called ahead and asked the hammam guardians if they would stay open later just for us. With classic Moroccan-style hospitality they readily agreed to wait for us to arrive around 8 p.m., their normal closing time.

Excitement was running high. Our first chore was to purchase hammam mitts from a pharmacy; we were told these were de rigueur for the hammam. Amina's counterpart on the trip, Ismael, gallantly purchased a red, rough single mitt for each of us.

At the appointed hour, we—twelve pale American women—arrived at the hammam. I was surprised that from the outside it was so unremarkable: a simple brick one-story building with a no-fuss hand-painted wooden sign near the entrance that simply read "Hammam." We entered a theatre-style booth to pay the equivalent of US $1.50 and were ushered into the women's side, while Ismael and Muhammad, the driver, retired to the men's section.

We were met by a buxom, dark-skinned, unveiled woman in a white djalaba and white apron, with a white cloth tied around her head. She pointed to benches along the wall and began to assist each of us in getting undressed. She undid bras, pulled down zippers, even took off socks and shoes. With twelve of us she had a busy time of it, but she managed to give some personal attention to everyone. We were told not to fold our clothes as she would gladly do that for us. She gave us each a white towel and a small bar of olive oil soap and fairly shoved us, one by one, into the bath proper.

We entered a large, steaming-hot room with plain white tiles over the floor, walls, and ceiling. No fancy arches, colored tiles, or Arabic music for us. Still, it was exciting to finally be here in a real hammam. Several other Moroccan women were in the steam room, each seated on a small stool on a carpet, surrounded by their bath supplies. Children frolicked with each other as their mothers bathed them from a rubber bucket of steaming water. Occasionally one of the women would let out a loud call of ululation that shattered the relative quiet.

Three attendants—of varying ages and sizes, wearing only panties—descended on us. After they had carefully scrubbed down the floor with soap and hot water, they made signs for each of us to sit down in a corner of the large room. There we sat, twelve naked, curious women, wide-eyed and speechless. No one seemed to mind our nudity in spite of the Muslim sanction against women showing skin in public.

Later, when we were told how unusual it was to be totally naked in the hammam, I felt quite embarrassed—but if they were upset at the time, they didn't show it.

Amina was not going to spoil the evening by giving us a lecture on the hammam; she sat quietly on the sidelines, performing her own ablutions with a sly smile on her face and, I thought, suppressing some giggles. Our three attendants scurried around like ants, hauling buckets of hot water from the adjoining room. Next, they unceremoniously threw the hot water on each of us, using one bucketful among three women. Then they generously slathered the olive oil soap into every nook and cranny of our travel-worn bodies.

With a bucket of water set in front of each of us, we looked at each other and asked, "Are we supposed to wash ourselves off now?" I reached for my bucket, but Amina broke her silence with a stern, "No, no, you do nothing." Then came the hilarious highlight. One by one, each of us was directed to lie down on the tile floor with her head in an attendant's lap. The attendant administered the most harsh and vigorous scrub with the hammam mitt, and oodles and streams of grunge and dirt rolled off. It was somewhat embarrassing, actually, as the ladies clucked and shook their heads in amazement at the filthy foreigners. As I looked up from my attendant's lap, her long, skinny, pendulous breasts slapped back and forth above my eyes, hitting my face, with no care for decorum whatsoever.

My scrubber lifted my arms and rubbed hard into my armpits, under my breasts, over my genital area, and finally down to my legs and feet. After a deep, painful massage on my feet, without warning she grabbed my ankles and flipped me over like a beached fish. This sudden move made each of us yelp and laugh. The attendant scrubbed the rest of the body in long strokes, leaving no crevice or fold untouched. The remaining families of women and children watched the performance gleefully, and all of us—locals, visitors, and scrubbers—surrendered to laughter. It was good-natured and totally fun.

Finally, when we were properly rubbed—and all amazed at how much dirt had come off our bodies—we were again treated to ablutions with buckets of water. Back and forth the attendants scurried, pushing and hauling the black rubber buckets from the unseen spigot. Three times in all we were doused, until they announced with satisfaction that we were now properly clean.

In the anteroom where we'd begun, the same attendant told us to sit and cool down before dressing. What fun it was to relate our amazement and delight to each other. We laughed until we cried. Eventually, the dressing-room lady helped us into our clean clothing and gave us very warm hugs. A peek inside revealed the hammam attendants gracefully scrubbing each other down as the end of a busy work day.

Outside, Ismael and Muhammad greeted their lobster-red, glowing, and very happy charges and chauffeured us to Amina's home, where her mother had prepared a late-night Moroccan feast in our honor.

—RA

Lady of the Waters © Brian Froud

The Celts, Druids, and Wiccans

Wells and the Womb of Life

The Celts arose out of the Indo-European culture that spread across Europe nearly 6,000 years ago, eventually settling in what is today Spain, France, and the British Isles.[1] They arrived in Britain around 500 B.C., where they became the ancestors of the modern Gaels, highland Scots, Irish, Welsh, Cornish, and Bretons.

The Celtic religion was based on the cycle of the seasons and nature. They worshipped spirits whom they believed resided in trees, mountains and lakes, rivers, and springs. Their pantheon was crowded with over 300 gods and goddesses, many of them related to water. The Great Mother Goddess represented fertility, creation, and the watery womb of chaos or formlessness. The goddess of healing waters, Sulis, had her temple on the site of present-day Bath, England, where hot springs gush forth to this day. The cloak of the god Manannan was woven from the sea and the waves were his horses. A magician, he provided sailors in need with a boat that obeyed their thoughts.[2]

Their places of worship were forest clearings or groves; they liked the dark, mysterious, secret feeling of being surrounded by their living gods. The very word "sanctuary" stems from their practice of worshiping in groves of trees. Springs, east-flowing rivers, and the confluence of rivers were also considered good locations for prayer and ceremony.[3]

Celtic beliefs eventually influenced the Catholicism that St. Patrick brought to Ireland, creating a Celtic Christian church that was more mystical, tolerant, and connected to nature than mainstream Catholicism. The Wiccan religion and contemporary Druidism grew out of pre-Christian Celtic beliefs.

69

The Druids

The Druids were the intellectual and spiritual elites of the pre-Christian Celts. The word druid is akin to a Gaulish word for tree and may stem from the Indo-European root *dreo-vid,* meaning "wise one," "knower," or "priest."[4] Some of the members of this ancient Celtic priesthood appear as magicians and wizards in Irish and Welsh sagas and popular Christian legends. Druids did not record their rituals, believing that the written word would bind up their beliefs and suffocate them. They preferred human recall, and priests memorized numerous long epic poems as part of their training. Revivals of Druid beliefs began in the seventeenth century, and adherents of contemporary revivals can be found worldwide, particularly in North America and the British Isles. Modern Druids are trying to reconstruct and revise the priestly traditions.

The Wiccans

Believers in the Wiccan religion are consciously trying to revise the folk traditions of magic that were practiced secretly in pre-Christian times, modeling themselves after wise village healers. The word *wicca* comes from the Anglo-Saxon word for wise. Based on the ancient ways of the goddess and mainly centered on women's spirituality, the Wiccan religion worships nature and honors the sacred female energy that pervades all of life. Most Wiccans believe in the God and the Goddess, known as the Lord and Lady. The female goddess is maiden, mother, and crone in one. These modern-day heirs to the mysteries of nature can be found worldwide, especially in North America and Britain. Wiccans are very connected to water and make frequent use of ritual baths.

Holy Wells

Springs and wells where water rises up from within the earth were revered as portals to the Otherworld, the womb of Mother Earth.[5] Shrines were often erected at these sites: The Celtic tomb-shrines of Britain are almost always found near wells or running water.

There are thousands of holy wells in the British Isles and Europe. The geography of the British Isles, in particular, is rich with springs, which often became the center of ritual and to this day are still venerated by villagers as humble and natural shrines. Even as late as the eighteenth century, resident priestesses assisted visitors to foresee their futures and fortunes in the movements of the waters.[6] Prophecy was also determined by the movements of leaves floating upon the water or fish swimming in the depths.[7]

Each holy well had a guardian or spirit who bestowed blessings and cures. Bathing in or drinking the well water could heal the sick. Well water could also bestow fertility. To curry the favor of the guardians and activate the power of the water, supplicants had to perform specific rituals, sometimes on certain days of the year, such as the pagan festivals of Beltane, Samhain, St. John's Night, and Midsummer's Eve. They walked in a circle around the well a certain number of times, offering chants and prayers. On some occasions, well water was drunk from a vessel such as a bowl hewn from oak, a clay jar, or a circular cup carved out of animal bone, reminiscent of cups carved out of human skulls by early Celts.[8] Carved representations of diseased organs or limbs were sometimes dipped into the well.[9] Afflicted parts of the body might be wiped with a rag dipped into the well water. The rag would then be hung up on a tree to rot.

To this day in England there is a custom of "well dressing." In addition to rags, villagers decorate wells with flowers, leaves, seeds, and other natural objects. In ancient times this was another way to thank the deity of the well for its good life-giving water and blessings.

The Celts are responsible for the origin of the proverbial "wishing well." The guardian spirits of the wells could be fish, eels, frogs, or mischievous faeries and piskies and supplicants had to be careful of their unpredictable and capricious habits. To gain favor and have their wishes granted, visitors threw in or left offerings such as flowers, coins, pins, food, and weapons. Archaeologists have discovered chariots, mirrors, cauldrons, and animals in wells and other sacred bodies of water. Because it was the custom to separate spiritual offerings from the everyday world by ritual breakage, these were all broken or damaged. Broken gifts were rendered unusable for humans and fit only for use by the supernatural.[10]

Cauldrons

We tend to think of cauldrons as huge pots in which witches brew magic mixtures for spells and incantations. They are much more! In nearly every mythology there is a miraculous vessel, a chalice, a sacred cup that is hewn from divine sources. These vessels—including cauldrons—engender transformations[13] and are considered symbols of the Great Mother's cosmic womb.

Among the Celts of Gaul and Britain, the Cauldron of Regeneration was the central religious mystery of reincarnation. Welsh bards thought the goddess Branwen, owner of the Cauldron of Regeneration, could resuscitate dead men by immersing them in the cauldron overnight. The powerful fairy queen, "the Lady of the Lake of the Basin," dwelt in a sacred lake from which her brother Bran the Blessed raised the cauldron later known as the Holy Grail.[14]

Studies have shown that water that comes from great depths within the earth picks up and dissolves trace minerals not usually abundant in surface water. Well water has been found to contain a high percentage of minerals, especially germanium, which may account for its healing properties.[11] Germanium-laden water has a higher percentage of oxygen, making it more energetic and more suitable for healing the sick.[12]

Wells were also sacred in other parts of the world. In northern Europe, wells were associated with Mother Hel, whose name gave rise to the words holy, health, and healing, and the name Helen. Many pagan springs were named Helen's Well. There is also a myth about a sacred well called Hileva (Hel-Eve): A divine queen used its magic waters to put her dismembered lover back together and made him live again.[15]

As Roman Christianity spread across Europe, the missionaries found that they couldn't suppress the old forms of nature worship connected to these holy water sites, so they went with the flow, often erecting Christian churches, temples, and shrines at the same spot. As a result, the original names of many sacred wells were replaced with the names of Christian saints.

Today, people still make pilgrimages to wells to pray. It is common to light incense and candles around the well and lay bunches of wildflowers tied with grass on the surface of the water.

SPIRITUAL BATHING RITUALS

Ritual Baths

Wiccans use baths to remove any negative energy the body may have accumulated during the course of a day, and to purify and charge the body prior to any magical endeavor.

The most common ingredients in Wiccan ritual baths are water and salt. Sea salt is preferred over common table salt, although some of the literature states that plain old tap water and table salt used with good, strong intention will bring results, too. Other herbs may be added for specific purposes; for instance, hyssop can be infused in the salt water for the purpose of clarifying thoughts and grounding oneself before entering into a ceremony or circle.

Wiccan Cleansing Bath

1 tablespoon sea salt
2 teaspoons fresh rosemary leaves
1 tablespoon rubbed sage
1 whole lavender flower

Pulverize the plants into a coarse mixture. Add salt. Place the mixture in a small cotton pouch and let it steep in very warm to hot bath water. Or boil the mixture in a quart of water in a covered saucepan for five minutes, filter, then pour the herbal tea into bath water. Light candles and soak for twenty minutes. Clear the mind and meditate on the ceremony to be conducted.

Bath to Block Negative Influences and Energy

1 tablespoon sea salt
1 whole lavender flower
3 whole marigold flowers

Crush the flowers into a coarse powder and add the salt. Place in a cotton pouch and steep in bath water, or boil in a covered saucepan for five minutes, strain if desired, and add to the bath water. Light candles. Soak for thirty minutes.

Eclipse Meditation and Bath

Solar eclipses, which always occur on the new moon, and lunar eclipses, which always occur on the full moon, are times when the energies of the moon are amplified and are traditionally good opportunities for a major transformation.[16] Many rituals have been created to take advantage of this powerful confluence. Here is one—

You will need:

A white candle
Salt
Purified or spring water
Incense
Small pieces of paper and a pen

Add hyssop and lavender or salt to your bath water. As you bathe, visualize any blocks and fears and release them. Affirm that you are ready to take yourself to the next level, then face the truth with an open heart and mind.

After your bath, sit in front of your altar, and practice basic grounding exercises and rhythmic breathing. Ground yourself by imagining your spine growing roots that grow down into the earth, and with each inhalation, breath in the energy from the core of the earth. With each exhalation, let go of fears, doubt, sadness, apathy, or whatever you need to release. The earth can turn almost anything into fertilizer, so transform your "negatives" into something you can use.

Drumming is another great way to find the rhythmic breathing essential for meditation. One of the fastest ways to reach the sleep stage alpha is to follow the tempo of the heartbeat with your drum.

Pour salt into a cup of water, and clear yourself by lightly sprinkling and anointing yourself with it.

Light a candle. Meditate on the symbolism of the flame—fire transforms and illuminates. Stare into the flame for a while and ask for clarity and truth during this eclipse cycle. Give yourself permission to release any and all thought forms that no longer serve your highest good.

1. a) Ask yourself: What area of my life needs some new ideas and a fresh perspective?

   b) Write down your answer on a small piece of paper, and create an affirmation supporting your new goal.

2. a) Ask yourself: How can I break through restrictive "safe" constructs, to be fully alive and, like the phoenix, be reborn through transformation?

b) Write down your answer on a small piece of paper, and create an affirmation supporting your new goal.

Save those pieces of paper for later.

3. On the remaining pieces of paper, write down, one to each piece of paper, whatever obstacles are keeping you from achieving your goals. Focus on each, then say something like:

> "All energy is neutral. I now release and transform this energy into an energy source that can be utilized for the highest good for all concerned."
>
> (or "in the name of Goddess / Universe / God / Creator" and so forth.)

Burn the paper, focusing on the transformation of the energy.

When you feel like you're clear, thank the deities, energies, spirits, guides, angels, and so forth you've worked with, bury the ashes in the earth, and imagine your goals for transformation fulfilled. Blessed Be.

From Sarolta G. DeFaltay[17]

Druid Herbal Water Rituals

The ancient Druids used vervain *(Verbena officinalis)* infused in water to sprinkle around altars and over people as a blessing. Bathing in vervain water was thought to give protection and to help make dreams come true.

Bathing in water infused with mistletoe *(Viscum album)* was thought to render the bather better able to perceive the Otherworld of spirits and faeries. The mistletoe that grew on their sacred oak trees was considered spiritually powerful and sacred.

From *A Druid's Herbal: For the Sacred Earth Year,* Ellen Evert Hopman.

At the Water's Edge Ritual

A waterfall would, of course, be ideal, but the key component is a body of flowing water in a clean and natural environment where the water has the opportunity to absorb and store energy from the sun, the earth, and plant life. You need only a vessel such as a wooden or glass bowl, a gourd, or even a bucket. Find a private place where you can be alone. (You can bring a close companion if this fits your needs). Try to choose the location and time such that you will not be distracted by insects.

Make yourself comfortable at the water's edge. Gaze undisturbed into the water and watch the flow and the sparkle of light playing on the moving water. Sit for a while, looking and listening. Try to empty your mind of thoughts, schedules, and to-do lists, concentrating on the meaning and the beauty of water, light, air, and earth around you. Feel yourself connected to every other living thing on Earth. Contemplate the greatness of God and Creation. Give thanks for the blessings in your life and count them, one by one. After twenty or thirty minutes, step into the water up to your knees. Pray according to your faith. Dip your vessel into the water and pour it over yourself from head to toe until you feel refreshed and renewed. With each dipping and pouring, ask that your worries, fears, and anxieties be carried away from you and be replaced with courage, faith, and fulfillment.

Wiccan Water Gazing Ritual for Guidance

For this ritual, still dark water is recommended: "from the womb of darkness you will uncover your answers." The ritual works best at night or dusk.

Reflect into the depths of a pond, water in dark bowl, or a tidepool for five to fifteen minutes, or longer if possible. Get as comfortable as possible. Unfocus your eyes, as if trying to find the image in a hologram. Relax your mind and allow thoughts to drift in and out of your awareness, without concentrating on any particular image or ideas. Try to become effortless in your search, open to solutions and random musings. Withdraw your eyes from the water when you feel uncomfortable or distracted, or feel intuitively that the time is at an end. If you did not receive a message, wait a couple of days and repeat the ceremony.

From *The Wicca Cookbook: Recipes, Ritual and Lore*, Jamie Wood and Tara Seefeldt

Blessing the Home with Holy Water and Salt: A Pagan Asperging Ritual

The word asperge is from Latin, "to sprinkle with holy water." This is an ancient ceremony, depicted on temple reliefs of ancient Babylon, where artichokes on stems were dipped in holy water to sprinkle on worshippers entering their temples.

This ritual is very effective for erecting spiritual boundaries to malign influences. It should be performed before moving into a new house, or after any negative event happens in a home, such as a robbery or violence. This ritual can also keep bad dreams away from children.

You will need:

Collected rainwater or spring water from a bottle
Salt, preferably sea salt
Sprig of a healing herb, such as rosemary, rue, or basil
A beautiful ceremonial plate and bowl
A #2 graphite pencil
A household broom

Place the water into the ceremonial bowl. Hold your hands over the water, palms down, and pray:

> *Blessed Water, Immortal One,*
> *You cycle as moisture, as vapor, as frost and snow, eternally.*
> *You rage as a river in flood and dream as a woodland spring.*
> *Your light is the Rainbow bent in Heaven.*
> *You are within me, essential to my life.*
> *I call upon You now to purify my home.*
> *So Mote It Be.*

Place the salt onto the ceremonial plate. Hold your hands over the salt, palms down, and pray:

> *Blessed Salt, Elemental Being,*
> *Crystal of Earth and Sea,*
> *You glitter in caves, dissolve in Seawater,*
> *You share Your strength generously,*
> *You purify wounds, preserve food,*
> *You are within me, essential to my life.*
> *I call upon You now to protect my home.*
> *So Mote It Be.*

With one quick gesture, tip the plate of salt into the bowl of water. Stir the salt and water together with the sprig of herb and pray:

> *Water and Salt conjoined, bring purity and strength to this home. Blessed*
> *Rosemary [or Rue, or whatever herb you have] assist Water*
> *and Salt in this work. Evict what is malign or impure. Purify and*
> *strengthen the walls, windows, and doors. Prevent any evil from entering*
> *this home, our sanctuary. In the Name of [your favorite deity],*
> *So Mote It Be.*

Begin at the top of the house. At every aperture, with your #2 graphite pencil draw a small version of your favorite deity's sacred symbol. It can be very small and discreet—on the side of the window frame, for example.

When you have drawn the sacred symbol, dip the sprig of herb into the consecrated water and salt, and say:

> *By the Power of Immortal Water,*
> *By the Strength of Elemental Salt,*
> *With the help of Holy Rue [or Rosemary, or Thyme]*
> *I ward this [window, door, etc.] in the Name of [your favorite deity].*
> *So Mote It Be.*

Make sure that you draw your symbol on every aperture, and don't forget things like the incoming water line, electric line, phone line, exhaust fan outlets, and so on. If you are doing this work after a violent event, and there is a mirror in the room in which the violent event occurred, draw your symbol, then sprinkle and pray over the mirror.

Move clockwise downstairs, including the basement, but omitting the front and back doors, until you have warded every other aperture in the house. Ward the back door second to last, and draw the symbol both inside and outside the door. Sprinkle the water and salt on the back steps as well as on the door itself, saying your prayers. Ward the front door last of all, inside and outside. Pour whatever remains of the water and salt mixture onto the front steps and sweep the water and salt down the path to your home with a broom. Your home is now well and truly warded.

From *Caroline Kenner, Washington, D.C.*

The Finns and Russians

Warmth in Frozen Lands

Ancient peoples knew that pouring water over hot rocks would create a billowing steam that cleared the lungs and was deeply relaxing for body, mind, and soul.

No one really knows whether the hot-air bath came from one source or developed indigenously in many places. Sweat lodges have been found all over the world—in central Asia, Turkey, Russia, Germany, Finland, the British Isles, North and South America, Africa, Melanesia, New Guinea, and Polynesia. However, the first recorded steam or vapor bath is attributed to a nomadic tribe in the Ukraine known as the Scythians. The Scythian bath consisted of a felt tent draped over a tripod made of sticks tied together at the top. Red-hot rocks were placed inside the tent and water containing hemp seed was tossed on the rocks. This early sweat bath was used for both physical healing and achieving an altered state in preparation for divine communion.

The Finns: The Soul of the Savusauna

When the Finns migrated north and west from Central Asia, they brought their portable sweat lodges along with them. Even when they gave up their nomadic ways in favor of farming, they held onto their bathing traditions. Even today, the most familiar of the hot-air baths, the Finnish sauna, remains an integral part of Finnish life from the cradle to the grave.

Although we may not think of saunas as having any spiritual meaning, they do! They are part of the lore of the ancient Finnish epic poem, the Kalevala. *Löyly,* the name for the steam created by throwing water over the rocks, originally meant soul or spirit.[1] It can be also be defined as spirit of life or steam. Immersion in the *löyly* was an experience beyond the ordinary that helped villagers transcend the worries of everyday life and protected them from disease and evil influences.

Understandably, ancient Finns living in a land of bitterly cold winters believed that fire was not only sent from heaven, it was heaven itself. As a result, they used choice firewood to fuel the fires of their ritual saunas. The old Finnish *savusauna* or "smoke sauna"—a structure built with logs, in which wood was burned to create the warmth—was the heart of village life.

Saturday-night baths in summer and winter were (and sometimes still are) very important communal events. Men, women, and children bathed together, unabashedly naked, slapping each other with vasta or vihta—birch twigs—to help the heat permeate deep into their pores. In the savusauna, they celebrated communal and private rituals and rites of passage. Women went through a purification ceremony in the sauna to prepare for marriage. Old people returned for one last sweat before they died.

The baths also served as an all-purpose infirmary. The tannic acid that leached from the wood that was burned created a germ-free environment. This made it the best place for women to give birth and for bloodletting and minor operations performed by early barber surgeons or the village apothecary. As an old Finnish proverb states, "The sauna is the poor man's apothecary." Even today, many elder Finns boast of having been born in the sauna.

The stubborn Finns refused to let Christian anti-bathing attitudes come between them and their löyly. But in the late eighteenth century, extensive use of public baths diminished as wood became scarce. At the same time, some doctors blamed the baths

The Shape-Shifting Water Spirit

Like many other peoples, the Finns once believed in water spirits with dark powers. Their folklore tells of a sinister creature that dwelled underwater in wells, springs, and rivers. Some called the creature by its Scandinavian name, Näkki; to others it was the *vedenhaltija* or, in eastern Finland, *vetehinen*. It could appear in any one of several guises, always naked: as a long-haired, bearded man; as a woman, standing in the water or sitting on a rock, washing and combing her long, dark hair; or as an animal or a devil. It was a dangerous force, not to be mocked, as it would try to coax people to a watery death.

for the spread of venereal disease; others said the inhalation of smoke caused convulsions, tumors, and premature loss of vision, and were especially harmful for children. Private showers and tubs became fashionable and the rich traveled by carriage to resorts to take the waters. However, many rural people still clung to their saunas.[2]

Interestingly, World War II contributed to the twentieth-century resurgence of the sauna. Finnish soldiers found the sauna so essential that they designed portable tents that were easily converted into saunas. Soldiers were de-loused and freezing troops warmed in these military tents. As it turned out, Finnish soldiers stayed healthier than other soldiers who were not so fortunate as to have brought along a steam tent. When the soldiers came home from the war, they sparked renewed interest in saunas. By then, the old-fashioned savusauna, with its need for massive amounts of precious wood, had been replaced by more efficient prefabricated structures with electric- and gas-heated stoves. Over half of the world's sauna sales today are in Finland, where there are two million saunas for five million people.

The Russians: Banniks in the Bania

Russian sweat baths also originated in central Asia, and share many characteristics with the Finnish sauna. Yet the Russian *bania* has a culture all its own, as can be seen in this early narrative penned by the Apostle Andrew in 1113:

> "Wondrous to relate, I saw the land of the Slavs, and while I was among them, I noticed their wooden bath-houses. They warm themselves to extreme heat, then undress, and after anointing themselves with tallow, take young reeds and lash their bodies. They actually lash themselves so violently that they barely escape alive. They then drench themselves with cold water, and thus are revived. They think nothing of doing this every day and actually inflict such voluntary torture upon themselves. They make of the act not a mere washing but a veritable torment."

Andrew focused on the dramatic and masochistic aspects of the bania ritual, ignoring its hygienic, pleasurable, and therapeutic qualities. In reality, bathers laid on hay-stuffed pillows as the scent of leaves and aromatic herbs wafted through the bania, and were washed and scrubbed by an attendant or companion. True, after drinking a libation of wine mixed with beer, they took turns beating each other with branches until their skins glowed flaming red, but this vigorous slapping stimulated circulation and forced the heat deep into their pores. Next came a dip in an icy creek or a roll in the snow, after which the bathers returned for another round of steam. Each bania session usually included four rounds of heating and cooling.[3]

"We all know how man came into being
Man was created when God took a bania and sweated profusely.
He dried himself off with straw and dropped the straw to earth
Where the Devil used the straw to create the body
Then later, God gave man his soul."

—RUSSIAN SORCERER, 1071

Men and women bathed together, even though the church heartily disapproved; bathers claimed that the monks and nuns themselves had promiscuous bathing habits and were no more chaste than the people.

Spirits in the Bania

Humans were not the only species that inhabited the bania. A common thread in many sweat-bath cultures is a fairy or spirit who dwells in the bath, and in Russia they are called the *banniks:* unpredictable spirits who live behind the stove or under the benches. Like most of their counterparts around the world, they have capricious natures, are sensitive to insults or misbehavior, and can be vengeful. These persnickety spirits even demand that the bania be kept clean and that they open on time.[4]

Banniks were elderly male spirits with long-nailed, hairy paws. They rarely showed themselves, except if they were very displeased by disrespect in the bania, such as sexual intercourse while bathing, or loud talking or swearing. The bannik could become particularly upset when strangers entered the bania; he might throw hot rocks or boiling hot water at them. To protect themselves from banniks, bathers made a sign of the cross before entering the bath and wished the other bathers a pleasant bath. Upon leaving, they gave the spirit a hearty farewell.

Curious souls who wanted to see a bannik had to enter the bania alone; with only one leg in, they would place a crucifix under the left foot as a sign of having rejected the Christian god. Then the bannik might show himself. He also expected a sacrifice from time to time, usually a black chicken that would be choked and buried under the building. Well into the early part of the twentieth century, when old banias were dismantled the remains of sacrificed chickens were found.

There were also benevolent bania spirits who could remove evil spells and wicked influences from bathers. They could even bestow magical powers to see the future, if one knew the proper ritual and offerings. Witches and sorcerers gathered together in banias to connect with these supernatural forces, and to increase their powers of divination and their ability to lift evil spells.

The magical and supernatural aspects of the Russian bania drew people to celebrate coming-of-age and nuptial ceremonies there. A bride's sweat was collected in the bania by pouring milk over her body, then coating her with flour. This flour was later incorporated in the wedding cake. Her sweat was also mixed with vodka, wine, and grains to be poured over the rocks. Honey and hops were added to water and poured over the hot rocks to ensure a rich, sweet life for her. Like their neighbor Finns, Russian women liked to give birth in the bania, and some ailing elders demanded to be carried to the bania so they could breathe their last in the hot clouds of steam.[5]

SPIRITUAL BATHING RITUALS

Where to Take a Russian Bath

St. Petersburg in Russia boasts more than 60 public bania. It is recommended that you bring your own towel, shampoo, plastic shoes, and a beer to fully appreciate the experience. You can buy a *venik* or leafy bunch of birch twigs with which to vigorously swat yourself and drive out the toxins. Don't be surprised if another bather offers to switch you and asks you to reciprocate.

Most bathers prefer to start with the dry sauna, then go to the steam room, where water containing eucalyptus oil is regularly ladled onto heated rocks to create fragrant and deeply cleansing steam. After a dip in the cold pool you might enjoy a cup of tea and some talk, then start all over again.

In case Russia is not in your travel plans, look for a Russian bath in just about any large city. One famous one on 10th Street on New York City's lower East Side was opened by Jewish immigrants from Russia in 1892. Over the years, the popularity of the *schvitz,* as it is known, has waxed and waned. Legend has it that during the days of the mafia rule, attendants had to be deaf so as not to overhear the conversations of gangsters and politicians who were regular patrons of the bath. Bathers can be vigorously massaged with a *platza* or broom made from oak leaves dipped in hot, soapy water. The 10th Street schvitz offers the classic cold-pool dip between rounds of steam and scrubbing. As a *Boston Globe* reporter put it, "Something happens when a group of grown men or women sit in a steam bath and attempt to wring themselves out to the last drop. The heat irons out nagging stresses and aches. The humidity subdues the mind. Everyone's circulation goes into high gear. Then the gabbing starts."[6]

Midsummer's Eve Magical Finnish Cure with Dew Water

Finnish folk custom has it that dew collected on Midsummer's Eve (the summer solstice) can heal wounds and infectious diseases. In the evening lay out a sheet on a lawn or meadow; by morning it should be drenched with dew. Wring out the dew into a vessel and wash yourself with it.[7]

The Sauna at Home

Home saunas have been popular for many years—and for good reason. The health benefits are well documented, and include improved immune function, better skin, and detoxification—plus great relaxation and enjoyment for every member of the family. If you have a sauna in your home, consider having a sauna theme party in conjunction with a special event celebration, such as a wedding shower. Follow the lead of the Finns, who treat the bride-to-be like a celebrity, offering richly scented gifts and marital advice. A sauna party could also fit nicely into a housewarming get-together or a mid-winter cold weather buster for your friends. Have your guests bring oversized towels and house slippers; read folk tales and serve drinks and food appropriate to Finland, Norway, and Sweden. If you can't find branches of birch leaves, try bay leaves. Get creative and have fun.

The Native Americans

Great Spirit and Shining Water

Long before the arrival of Europeans, the native peoples of the Americas practiced various forms of spiritual bathing for health and ritual purification. They honored water as one of the major sources of life.

Some European settlers, coming from a culture unaccustomed to regular bathing, marveled at the daily habits of the Native Americans, who cleansed themselves in cold rivers and streams even in mid-winter. Chronicles abound with tales of white Europeans cured of all manner of diseases by the Native Americans who administered sweat baths to them.

Sadly, the open-mindedness of a few didn't help Native Americans hold onto their lands or traditions. Government officials, anxious to gain control over the fiercely independent tribes, saw Native American spiritual bathing as a threat. The religious overtones of the sweat-lodge ceremony elicited the wrath of the church. It wasn't long before Native Americans were forbidden to enter a sweat lodge.

Fortunately, a few tribes managed to hold on to their sweat-lodge traditions, and since the 1970s the sweat lodge has been enjoying a revival. It is once again a living spiritual tradition that can be experienced by Native American and non-Native American alike.

"The sweat lodge utilizes all powers of the universe: earth, and things that grow from the earth; water, fire, and air. The warm, dark, moist ambience inside a sweat bath is easily likened to a womb, even the womb of Mother Earth herself. A tired, dirty bather climbs into the confines of the sweat bath, crouches in a fetal position, sweats out impurities and emerges refreshed and cleansed—reborn."

—BLACK ELK, LAKOTA ELDER

Sacred Ceremony

Native American tribes, dwelling in harmony with the land, made no distinction between spirit, mind, and body. It was their custom to teach their children that the spiritual life deserves and needs as much attention and healing as the physical.

Nowhere is this more evident than in the sweat lodge. Known by many names—the Lakota called it *inipi*[1]—the sweat is intended to bring about spiritual renewal of the soul and purification of the body, and to provide peace and relaxation for the mind. The sweat lodge is a place of refuge from the cares of everyday life: a place to receive guidance, healing, and dream visions from ancestor spirits and the Great Spirit.

The sweat is also part of the glue that holds communities together. Even today, some tribes hold sweats in honor of births and deaths, and when an individual passes from childhood to puberty, puberty to adulthood, being single to marriage, barrenness to fertility, or illness to health. At these times people need to draw closer to each other, to their ancestors, and to the Great Spirit, to help make the transition peaceful and meaningful. In the old days, hunters visited the sweat lodge to purge themselves of human odors that might be picked up by their prey. Warriors visited the sweat lodge after battles to purify themselves before returning to domestic life.

No two Native American tribes have exactly the same spiritual bathing tradition, but for all tribes every aspect of the sweat bath is sacred: the preparation, each element carried into the lodge, and every word and action taken by the lodge keeper and ceremony participants.

As the symbol of Earth Mother's womb, the sanctity and ceremonial purity of the sweat lodge is paramount. Like any womb, it cannot produce a healthy offspring if it is contaminated with improper influences and emotions. It is important for all bathers to be on an equal social footing and to shed all pretenses, as well as negative emotions such as anger and jealousy, before entering. Alcohol and drugs are not permitted, nor anything that is not natural—jewelry, watches, glasses, false teeth, contacts, cosmetics, hairpins, and the like. Some tribes don't allow women to enter the sweat lodge during menstruation.

The entrance to the lodge always points east, where Father Sun lives, and is at ground level so that bathers must crawl in on their hands and knees, reflecting on their own humility. As they crawl from east to west, following the path of the sun, they repeat a prayer of invocation, usually "All my relations," or *"Matakweyasin,"* signifying the connectedness of all the elements of the sacred lodge and the bathers.

In some traditions, the bathers prepare a prayer twist before entering the lodge. The prayer twist is made of four colors: red, white, yellow, and black, symbolizing the four races of humanity and the four sacred directions and their divine characteristics. While preparing the prayer twist, the bather prays and meditates on the desired result of the sweat experience.

Most bathers enter the lodge naked, but a light wrap or towel is permitted. Some bathers throw an offering of sage or other herbs on the fire when they enter. The lodge keeper is the last to enter and stays by the entrance flap so that he or she can open it if anyone inside feels faint or needs fresh air.

The sweat begins when the first water is poured over the heated, glowing rocks and the lodge keeper calls in the sacred energies needed for the desired outcome. In all, four rounds of sweat are performed. Seven rocks are carried in by the fire tender for each round. In between rounds, or when the when the heat becomes too intense, bathers may ask to be let outside for a "breather" or the entire group may jump into a cool stream.

During the ritual, bathers gain hope and strength from each other. A "talking stick," usually made of cedar or willow, is passed around so that each person has a chance to speak individually. No one may interrupt the person who holds the talking stick. Group chanting, praying, and singing are common and enhance the community feeling.

Many take this opportunity to make confessions, in an effort to relieve the heaviness and burdens of their spirit. Faith, honesty, and humility are the spiritual framework inside the lodge. The presence of sacred spirits washes away both physical and spiritual pain. Sometimes a flute is played, representing the Creator's first gift to man, the bird song. A sacred pipe filled with tobacco may be passed from east to west as each person says, "All my relations."

At the conclusion of this powerfully sacred and transformational experience, the bathers crawl out on their hands and knees, then dip themselves in a refreshing cool stream or roll in snow. If they entered as strangers, they leave as family.

The Sacred Elements

Although rituals and symbols differ from tribe to tribe, most elements of the sweat lodges are universal. The structures, large or small, are usually round or oval shaped as a symbol of rebirth from the womb or the earth mother.

The Gift of Water

Native Americans believe that water nourishes, heals, and sustains; it is a divine gift from the Creator. They recite prayers of thanksgiving to water when it is gathered from spring, river, or creek. Before the water is carried inside the lodge, a libation is poured onto Mother Earth in front of the lodge. Leaves from plants such as cedar, pine, and eucalyptus are sometimes added to the water, which may be passed around for sipping, accompanied by prayers of gratitude to the spirits of the plants.

The Healing Willow

Custom demands that when wood is gathered to build the frame of the bathhouse, no trees may be felled or harmed by cutting off branches; only dead or fallen wood may be used. Fallen or dry branches of the willow tree are commonly tied together with rawhide and may be covered with bark, grass, and skins of bear, moose, or—in olden days—bison. The willow branches are placed to honor the four directions of the universe, conceived of as spiritual forces that require reverence and remembrance. Willow bark contains salicin, a pain-reducing substance that is the active ingredient in aspirin. It is likely that the salicin-infused vapor from the willow branches is a good pain reliever for the bathers.

Fire's Perpetual Light

The firewood is honored with thanks, then smudged with sage or cedar before the fire is started. Firewood represents the combination of the earth from which the tree grew, the sun that nourished it, and the rain that enlivened it. In the lodge, its sun/fire energy is released to warm the bones of Mother Earth. The fire is a piece of the sun, a symbol of the Creative Force. Representing the perpetual light of the world, it is a source of life and power. Damp or wet wood should not be used for the fire because this would bring together opposite spiritual elements: fire and water. For the same reason, one should not blow moist breath or spit onto the fire; instead, a fan or hat is used.

The Bellybutton of Mother Earth

In the center of the lodge, a small shallow pit may be dug to receive the heated rocks. This hole represents the center of the universe and, to some tribes, the bellybutton of Mother Earth. Dirt from digging the pit is piled up outside the lodge to be used as an altar where bathers may place their ceremonial amulets or objects that may help them during the sweat. The lodge keeper usually places offerings or ceremonial objects on the altar before the sweat begins, to enhance the presence of the spirit guides.

Rocks: Bones of the Earth

Twenty-eight melon-sized rocks are collected from dry fields, hillsides, or mountains, while traditional prayers or medicine songs are chanted. Rocks from streams or damp areas, and those containing quartz or white granite are never used because when the stored water within them expands with heat, they explode. The rocks are heated in an outside altar-fire and brought into the lodge pit seven at a time. Each rock is dedicated to a deity—the Creator, Mother Earth, Father Sun and each of the four directions—before water is thrown on it. The sacred rocks represent the bones of Mother and Grandmother Earth and the human relationship with matrilineal ancestors. They absorb the power and spirit of the fire and are a reminder of the penetrating goodness and warmth of the Creator. The water splashed on the rocks is holy, and the vapor is the visible symbol of the Creator's breath.

Sweat Chants and Prayers

Lodge keepers and pipe bearers are taught special chants for use during the sweat, which they may pass on to one person in their lifetimes.[2] The lodge keeper also recites prayers for the bathers and gives thanks to the wood, fire, water, rocks, and other deities. Prayers and songs are appropriate at any time during the sweat. These may be old medicine songs handed down from grandmothers or popular songs with special meanings. Songs and prayers help bathers release their physical, emotional, and spiritual baggage, past and present. Prayers for peace, the planet, and the end of suffering in the world are common.

A SPIRITUAL BATHING RITUAL

Where to Experience a Sweat

Sweat lodges are now held all over the United States; take a look on the internet for one near you. You can also build a sweat lodge. The simplest kind is made from three sticks, about eight to ten feet long, set up like a tripod and bound at the junction. This frame is covered over with blankets, felt, skins, or any natural material that has not been treated with chemicals. A natural-fiber bottomless pup tent is always a good portable sweat lodge, but has room for only two or three people. Larger lodges should be constructed in the typical egg shape.[3] The prayers, songs, and ceremonial rituals are vital to the sanctity and success of a sweat lodge, so some Native Americans say that without the presence of a medicine person or spiritual leader it is not an authentic tribal sweat.[4]

Hippie Dip

Years ago, deep in the California High Sierra outside of Yreka, I was a member of the Blackbear commune, started by a group of folks looking to live a freer, alternative lifestyle. We were close neighbors with a Native American tribe that was friendly and supportive of our philosophy of organic gardening, living off the land, and pooling our mutual resources. The tribal members often came to Black-bear to ask us to participate in their sacred sweat lodges. I was born and raised a Catholic and had still had very little exposure to other cultures. The hippie dropout revolution was already way exotic and adventurous for me, a former advertising executive from Chicago.

One cool summer night, our First Nation neighbors graciously set up a full-scale Native American sweat lodge expressly for our benefit and spiritual renewal. I remember asking around what it would be like; I couldn't garner much response beyond, "Oh, man, it's really far out. You'll *love* it. Totally groovy."

A group of men had built an enormous (by Native American standards) sweat lodge. A makeshift geodesic dome, about nine feet high and twelve feet in diameter and covered with white plastic sheets, it could easily shelter thirty or forty people.

One full-moon night in August, after the fire had been stoked for hours to heat the rocks, the ceremonial blowing of a conch shell sounded. I gathered my towel, my shower shoes, and my five-year-old son and made my way up the hill in a moonlit procession of drumming and chanting mountain folks, all ready to experience the sweat lodge together.

We stripped off our clothes, and each left a little offering at the makeshift altar outside the entrance to the lodge. Some left tobacco; others, bags of stones or herbs; still others, only heartfelt prayers of gratitude for our gardens and organic food. I deposited a handful of sunflower seeds recently harvested by my class of students in our one-room school house, in which I served as the sole teacher. I gave my thanks for the harvest and for the great fun-filled time the children had had harvesting the yellow-headed giants and then building a little clubhouse from the stalks with the help of some of their fathers.

I stepped from the cool night air into a blast of moist heat. It hit my face and body in currents that were at first frightening, then comforting. Men, women, and children gathered together and formed a circle. Once we were all in and settled, the chief attendant signaled for the outside flap to be closed. With a series of prayers, he threw the first dipperful of water onto the hot rocks, which emitted a blast of steam that gradually wafted around the circle. He told us that each dipperful was for a spirit of nature and that we should concentrate on the spirit of fire, air, water, and earth as he turned in a circle to honor the four directions.

I sat in a veritable sea of exposed and naked humanity. Some stood; others sat. A few, who were almost immediately distressed by the heat, were instructed to lie down on the tarp-covered earth where it was the coolest. Soon, rivulets of sweat began to run down my body to collect in a pool where I sat. I was shocked by the amount of sweat and saw how others began to rub their bodies with their own hands to release layers upon layers of grease and grime. I, who shower and bathe daily, was surprised to see how much accumulated grunge I was harboring on my skin.

While the water splashing and chanting continued, I rubbed and rubbed, peeling off black residue all over my sweat-drenched body. The first round finished with more prayers and a temporary opening of the flap to allow us to breathe some fresh, cool air for a few minutes. Then the second round of sweating, splashing, chanting, and prayers began. This time we were each given an opportunity to cleanse our souls by speaking from the heart about some-thing we would like to be cleansed of, such as an old hurt, an insult, a theft, or whatever transgression had been committed. That was hard for some; impressively smooth for others, myself among them. I was surprised by how easy it was to express an old grief and ask for help in letting it go, and how deeply accepting and empathic I felt with each person's "confession." The children had left after the first flap opening and could be heard outside, splashing in the creek.

Finally, after the fourth round of sweating, it was over and we all ambled out to jump into the ice-cold mountain creek, made muddy by the children's water games. Looking up at the night sky and the blinking stars, I truly felt relieved of emotional, physical, and spiritual weight. I felt a sense of peace and a pervading love and deep reverence for all of creation. We were brothers and sisters under the sky, caressed by the gurgling water, our way lighted by the moon. We were one with the Great Spirit.

—RA

The Maya

In Search of Spiritual Healing

Famed for the ruins of their great cities, such as Tikal and Palenque, the Maya peoples have dwelled in Central America for thousands of years. Although many of their traditions were stamped out by zealous Spanish Catholic missionaries in the 1500s, their spiritual bathing practices survived, passed by word of mouth from mother to daughter, elder to apprentice.

Even today, spiritual bathing is an integral and revered component of indigenous Maya medical practices and village life. Adults and children are regularly bathed in water infused with sacred plants and prayers to ensure their emotional, spiritual, and physical well-being. These baths, respected by local medical doctors, now face a new threat: Christian missionaries from fundamentalist churches believe that ancient Maya rites are a form of demon worship.

Maya ritual baths are designed to treat what the Maya call spiritual diseases of the soul. These diseases encompass the universality of all human suffering. For example, the spiritual illness *susto* can be compared to fright or trauma. *Tristeza* is sadness or depression. *Pesar* is grief due to loss through death, fire, or natural disasters, and *invidia* is envy and jealousy that streams out from one person to affect others.

Each spiritual illness has a specific set of symptoms that may include general malaise, stomach upsets, insomnia, nightmares, nervousness, and a lack of interest in daily affairs of life. People with a spiritual disease may also feel dispirited, weak, fragmented, and disassociated from themselves and the world.

Why do spiritual illnesses occur? The Maya, like many other peoples around the globe, believe that each person's soul is made up of vital energy, which they call *ch'ulel*. Everything created by the gods has been imbued with *ch'ulel* from the beginning of time.[1] Spiritual illnesses cause the loss of *ch'ulel*—what shamans of other cultures refer to as soul loss. The Maya believe that souls can be frightened away, wander off, or even be abducted, and that treatment with bathing, prayers, plants, and incense can lure the soul back into the physical body.

To call back the soul, Maya healers select from hundreds of different flowers, leaves, roots, and tree barks in season to prepare their healing baths. The specific plant or prayer chosen depends on the ailment and the symptoms. For instance, marigold is the herb of choice for traumatized infants or children. Basil and rue are good additions to the baths of adults suffering from envy and jealousy. Flowers of the belladonna plant are used to bathe those who cannot sleep or who have recurring nightmares. The plants may be boiled in water or soaked in the sun for a few hours. They may be administered as a steam bath, a sitz bath, or a foot bath, or by pouring the plant-water mixture over the entire body.

The number of plants chosen for a bath is also important. Numbers represent deities and spiritual concepts to the Maya. Some healers collect four flowers, or four leaves from four different plants while saying four prayers. Others prefer the numbers three, seven, or nine. Nine and four are probably the most commonly used numbers in Maya spiritual healing. Nine is popular because in the Maya cosmic view there are nine levels of the Underworld, Nine Benevolent Spirits, and Nine Lords of the Night.[2]

Prayer

Prayer is the foundation on which Mayan spiritual healing is built. Prayers are said while collecting plants, while preparing the water-plant mixture, and during the baths. Maya prayers today include a heavy dose of Christianity, thanks to the influence of the Catholic church.

The Herb Collector's Prayer (translated into English from Mayan)

Plants to be used for spiritual bathing *must* be collected with prayer and care. We include the herb collector's prayer that Maya healers use while collecting plants to be used in ritual baths. We are indebted to Don Elijio Panti, Maya shaman of Belize (1893-1996), for sharing this prayer with us.

"In the name of the Father, the Son and the Holy Spirit, I give thanks to
the spirit of this plant and I have faith with all my heart that you will
help me to make a healing, purifying bath for [person's name]."

Maya spiritual baths are thought to be most powerful when taken on a Thursday
or a Friday. One shaman has explained that these are the days that the Nine Benevolent
Spirits are believed to wander the earth to hear the prayers of the faithful. However,
prayers are answered seven days a week.

Incense

The earliest Spanish chronicles relate stories of soldiers and missionaries being
met by Maya priests, smudged with incense and carrying incense burners. Since
ancient times, the Maya have considered incense a good *ch'ulel* carrier. Maya healers
say the *ch'ulel* in the incense bathes the environment and the energy body surrounding a person. The Maya favor the incense of copal resin (*pom*) and dried rosemary
leaves for treatment of all spiritual ailments. Incense is usually used in combination
with baths.

Maya Sweat Lodges or *Zumpul-che*

Zumpul-che is the ancient Mayan term for sweat bath; it has been very much a part
of Maya life since earliest times. Recent excavations at Tikal and El Paraiso have
uncovered sweat house ruins—some believed to be over 1,200 years old. The ruins at
Piedras Negras have eight sweat baths. Murals on the North Temple of the ball court
at Chichén Itzá show that that Maya ball players may have undergone purification
rites in the sweat baths before the game.

Like their neighbors and successors, the Aztecs, the Maya respected the steam
bath's efficacy for treating both physical and spiritual diseases. To bring about a trance
state, the Maya favored a combination of heat, sweat, prayers, and fasting, sometimes
with the help of hallucinogenic drugs. And as the Aztecs would later do, Maya kings
and priests took sweat baths before engaging in religious rituals with the gods to ask
for blessings.

Today, villagers and healers descended from the Maya still use sweat baths—now
known as *bajos*—for themselves and patients to treat a variety of ailments, including
those considered to be of supernatural origin.

Cenotes

The Mayan gods bestow water in the form of springs, wells, rivers, lakes, and rain. The Maya who lived in the Yucatan have no rivers or lakes; they consider *cenotes*—the underground water that collects in sinkholes caused by the collapse of soft limestone soil—to be sacred. Some of these are accessible to the public.

One of the best-known cenotes, known as the Well of Sacrifice, is at Chichén Itzá. For hundreds of years, pilgrims from all over the Maya world traveled to this sacred water site. Once there, they cast into its depths various offerings to the gods thought to dwell within. The Maya thought of the Well of Sacrifice as the navel of the world and the entrance into the Underworld, abode of the gods—especially the god of death, Yum Cimil. Sacrifices were made there to appease the gods so they would allow the rains to fall, crops to grow, and life to continue. In the late 1890s, the well-known American archaeologist Edward Thompson bought the hacienda on which the ruins of Chichén Itzá are located for five hundred dollars. He dredged the famed oval-shaped cenote to retrieve treasures buried there by the Maya.

Excavations have revealed copper bells, a common ornament of Yum Cimil; gold ornaments; jade beads; throwing sticks; and bits of textile. The most abundant objects are clay vessels filled with copal resin, often shaped into the form of a heart and painted blue—the color the Maya painted their sacrificial offerings. Also recovered from the Well of Sacrifice were human remains, believed to be sacrifices offered during times of famine, drought, or epidemic.

The Water Gods and the Rain Ceremony

Whether the Maya lived in the highlands, the coastal lowlands, or the dense jungles, they considered male and female water and rain gods to be major deities. Even today, some Maya still dedicate songs, dances, ceremonies, and supplications to the rain god Chac in the hope he will bring rain.

Chac's consort was Ix Chel—the goddess of the moon, bodies of water, childbirth, healing, and weaving. Much revered still, her name means Lady Rainbow or Sacred Feminine Translucent Light. Often prayers are addressed to her in the belief that she can convince her husband to do what the people ask. Ix Chel may be depicted in her guise as the goddess of weaving—as a maiden goddess kneeling in front of a loom—or as an elderly crone with an upturned clay pot of rainwater from which a glowing

Opposite: Swimming in a cenote in shaft of sunlight. Dzitnup, Yucatan, Mexico.

rainbow emerges. She is also associated with floods. On the last page of one of the few surviving ancient Maya books—the Dresden Codex—Ix Chel appears in her less gentle aspect as the goddess of death and destruction, holding her clay pot upside-down and sending a flood to destroy the world.

The rain ceremonies of today are probably not much changed from ancient times, except for the invocation of certain Christian saints. An altar of sticks and vines is built in the village or cornfield; this becomes symbolically the center of the earth. Celebrants first bathe in water infused with sacred plants and prayers. Then, women prepare an offering of corn *atole* (soft cooked corn meal) to set out on the altar in nine gourd bowls for the Nine Maya Spirits. A container of wine made from honey and "virgin water" from a deep natural well is also placed on the altar. (According to the ancient text of the Maya, the Popul Vuh—the Maya gods—made humans out of corn and water. The dough is said to be the flesh of humanity and the original waters of Creation, human blood. This is why ceremonial offerings to the gods usually include corn and water.[3])

At the four corners of the altar, four little boys are placed in a kneeling position to represent the *bacabs* who hold up the four corners of the earth. Copal is burned, prayers are recited to Chac, and the participants all make loud, roaring noises like thunder. Fresh, clean water is sprinkled on the four little boys, who then make frog sounds.[4]

Itz

Maya scholars David Friedel and Linda Schele describe the Maya concept of *itz,* which refers to sacred fluids, secretions, and liquids. *Itz* is powerful in that it is a direct gift and blessing from the spirits and can take many forms.[5] *Itz* can be a liquid or essence of something such as morning dew, semen, or human tears. The dripping water inside a cave is especially revered. *Itz* can also be found in the nectar of flowers, human sweat, and, especially, the wax that drips from votive candles. The wax is known as *yiitz kab,* the flowing liquid of heaven. Rain is the *itz* of the sky god, the primordial divine gift that sustains life.

HOW TO PREPARE A MAYA SPIRITUAL BATH AT HOME

A Summer Bath with Fresh Plants

Collect the following plants, reciting the herb collector's prayer several times (see page 100).

9 sprigs rue, about 6 inches long
9 stems marigold, with flowers, about 12 inches long
4 stems basil, about 12 inches long
or
4 stems motherwort, about 12 inches long
9 stems sage, about 12 inches long
9 stems Saint John's wort, about 12 inches long

Fill your washtub or your largest pot with water. Place the plants in the water and squeeze them between your hands. This is a good time to pray for what you wish to accomplish with this bath. Say what feels right and comes from the heart.

Breathe deeply and gratefully of the aroma, for this too is healing. After ten minutes or so, when the plants are well crushed and the water has taken on color and aroma, set it aside for one to eight hours. You can make this preparation in the morning and bathe that night, or you can prepare it in the evening and bathe in the morning.

If you have a bathtub, fill it half full with tap water at a temperature of your liking. Then scoop a half-cup of the herbal water out of the pot and drink it. Pour the remainder of the herbal water into the tub. You can strain out the leaves and flowers first if you wish to make cleaning up easier, but it is lovely to bathe surrounded by floating flowers and leaves. Some people pour all the plants into the tub and gather them up in their hands to rub over their face and body.

Soak for thirty minutes, relaxing and meditating on the purpose of the bath. Burn copal incense. This is a good time to pray.

If you have no bathtub, carry the pot of herbs into the shower. Sit on a stool or chair in the shower and use the bowl to slowly pour the herbal water over your body. You can add hot tap water to the pot of herbs for a warmer bath. To avoid clogging the drain, protect it with a strainer.

If it's warm enough to let your body air-dry rather than toweling off, do so; you'll gain the greatest possible benefit from the herbs.

A Winter Bath with Dried Plants

If fresh herbs are not available, use one cup of dried herbs—either a single herb or a combination—for each gallon of water. Try dried rosemary, sage, thyme, oregano, marigold flowers, lemon balm, or roses. Boil in a large pot for five minutes, then let steep for an hour. Pour into a bathtub partially filled with comfortably warm water and soak for twenty to thirty minutes.

Basil Floor-Washing Ritual

The Maya fill a bucket with water in which basil leaves have been squeezed and steeped, then dip a broom in it and sweep the stairs and entranceway to their home. They do this to ward off envy and also when they are feeling down on their luck.

Perform the basil-water sweep for nine consecutive days, starting on a Thursday or a Friday. Basil water can also be sprinkled all around the house, especially where you sleep, eat, and rest. While sprinkling the water, say out loud:

> "All bad luck must now leave me and this place. I have faith with all my heart that this sacred water and these prayers will dispel all misfortune and change my life for the better."

Maya Emotional Release Steam Bath

The *bajo* or clearing bath is best done at home with a family member or close friend. Teamwork is necessary to bring about this release. The one who prepares the bath should collect four, seven, or nine different fresh herbs while praying for the person who is to receive the steam bath. A mother might pray for the emotional healing of her child; a wife or husband, for their spouse; a confidant, for a friend. This can be a truly powerful way to release anger or memories of past hurts, recurring nightmares, or to help a person overcome a negative influence such as drugs.

It is best to choose aromatic herbs or those with which you have a special affinity. Some suggestions are basil, marigold, St. John's wort, oregano, thyme, rosemary, hyssop, lemon balm, and motherwort. While picking the herbs, pray for the person in need of emotional release and transformation, addressing these prayers to your deity and giving thanks to the plants for their cooperation.

Squeeze the gathered herbs into a pot of water with at least a two-gallon capacity. Crush the herbs well; the water should turn green. Again, while doing this, transmit your intention into the act by asking that the recipient be relieved of painful memories and cleansed of emotional and spiritual negativity. Place the pot on the stove, cover well, and boil for five minutes.

If the day is warm without drafty breezes, the steam bath can take place outside; otherwise, it's best done in the shower or bathroom. While the herbs boil, make the bather as comfortable as possible in a chair with a slatted or cane seat so that the steam can penetrate easily. Wrap the bather completely in blankets, with only the head left exposed, so that no heat can escape.

Remove the pot of boiling herbs from the stove and place it under the chair. Allow the bather to sit with the steam rising up through the slatted chair for twenty to thirty minutes. This should create profuse sweating. He or she should contemplate the issues at hand and be willing to allow the painful memories to surface for final purification and purging.

When finished, cover the bather well with a fresh, clean robe and socks to prevent drafts and cool air from entering the pores, which can cause muscle spasms.

This bath often draws tears, expressions of deep feelings, and a long verbal release. This is good and desirable; talking is part of the release, and the bather needs the helper to listen patiently and not try to psychoanalyze. The bath can be repeated as often as necessary, but no more than once or twice a week.

Maya Citrus Blossom Bath for the Full Moon

If you live in an area where citrus trees grow, you will love this bath made with the fresh, aromatic flowers from any citrus tree: orange, lemon, lime, grapefruit, or citron. These powerful baths clear away negative states, such as feeling attacked by others, feeling jealousy from others, and feeling emotionally or spiritually exhausted.

To glean the best potential spiritual clearing energy from the flowers, plan your bath for the time of the waxing moon—this is when flowers are said to reach their peak of aroma and fruiting potential. Traditional Maya healers recommend this bath be repeated nine times: three baths before the full moon phase, three baths during the full moon, and three as it begins to wane. Nine baths in nine days is the ideal, but if you can't fit them all in, take three baths any time during those nine days. Even just one can be beneficial if that's all that time allows.

During the day, when at least a few hours of sunlight remain, gather a handful of citrus blossoms, being sure to say a prayer of faith and thanksgiving while picking. Be gentle with the flowers; they fall apart easily. Remember that the tree is truly giving you a gift of itself and a potential fruit.

Place the blossoms in a basin of water in the sun for a few hours. Late in the afternoon or in the evening, pour the flower water over yourself while praying for the desired outcome. Or pour the flower water into your bath and soak for as long as you like, enjoying the delightful aroma and floating flowers. Meditate, contemplate, and *relax*.

A Shaman Gives a Maya Spiritual Bath

During my apprenticeship with the late Don Elijio Panti, I watched him prepare the plants for many patients' spiritual baths. I couldn't wait to try one of the baths myself. Finally, one day I had the opportunity when Don Elijio announced that it was time to perform the sacred Maya ceremony of the *Primicia* in order to introduce me as his disciple to the Nine Maya Spirits.

During the ceremony, he explained, he would speak to the spirits about me and ask that they give me every consideration they would give to him. To prepare me for the presence of the Spirits, he had to ritually bathe me. "They do not mean to do harm," he told me, "but if one is not prepared properly, the power of their presence can be harmful." He said that the bath was also intended to protect me from evil influence for the rest of my life.

On the appointed day, Don Elijio arrived at my home at Ix Chel Farm in the Cayo district of Belize. He had with him in an old plastic flour sack holding all the sacred items he would need for the ceremony. Then he and I walked into the forest surrounding my farm to collect the sacred plants for the bath.

This is a memorable moment in my life. Together we meandered through the forest, shaded by the canopy of trees above us, teased by butterflies, and serenaded by various bird calls. He would point with his gnarled, scarred finger at the plant he wanted me to collect, and together we said the thank you prayers. He spoke in Mayan; I, in Spanish. I could hear him say my name in his prayers; this was thrilling and made me feel honored and blessed.

When we had collected the nine plants, we walked back to the kitchen, where he filled a bucket with water and instructed me to sit next to him on the doorstop. He showed me how to crush the leaves and flowers between my hands until they were all quite a swirl of greenish brown. When I gathered up a bunch of the crushed plants in my hands and lifted it to my face, the aroma was wild and spicy and sweet, all at the same time. We placed the bath water in the sun to soak.

An hour before the ceremony was to begin, Don Elijio said it was time to take the spiritual bath. My son, Jimmy, carried the bucket to a little clearing under the ceiba tree (the kapok tree, sacred to the Maya) at the back of the farm. Don Elijio and I followed behind.

I wore a bathing suit and sat on a wooden chair. Don Elijio first said the nine Maya prayers: three prayers over each of my wrists and three while holding my head in his hands. Then he dipped into the bucket with a gourd bowl he had brought along just for this purpose and began pouring water over my head one bowl at a time. The water felt quite warmed from the sun as it cascaded down over my head, chest, and legs. Don Elijio chanted in Mayan the whole time. I sat in contemplative silence, trying to be as present and calm as possible while opening my heart to his beloved spirits and promising also to be of a pure heart, to respect them and their healing traditions, and to be the very best apprentice I could possibly be. When all of the water was finally poured over me, Don Elijio left me to sit alone. He suggested that I sit on the earth while my skin dried.

As I sat, I had the sensation that something was moving through my body down into the earth. It was as if a zipper ran through my flesh and some of my energy was being absorbed by the ground beneath me. For that moment, there was peace within and peace without. I felt welcomed by the Spirits, grateful, and humbled by the love around me.

—RA

The Aztecs

Communing with Gods

Aztec civilization flourished in the heart of the Mexican highlands from the thirteenth century until the arrival of the Spanish in the fifteenth century. The highland climate is very dry or very wet, depending on the season, so the Aztecs needed to devise clever ways to communicate with their deities—in particular, the moody rain god, Tlaloc, and his wife, the water goddess Chalchiuhtlicue.

One way of communicating with their many gods—including the two principal gods, Quetzacoatl and Tezcatlipoca—was through the *temezcal* or house of steam. The Aztec king and queen used the *temezcal* for ritual purification, before engaging in religious ceremonies during which they would communicate with the gods and the ancestor spirits, seek blessings for their people, and ask for assurance that the rain would continue to fall, the sun to rise, and the crops to grow.

Akin to the Native American sweat lodges and the Mayan *zumpul-che,* the temezcal is home to Aztec rituals that improve spiritual, mental, and emotional health. It was and still is a favorite remedy for almost every ill.[1] The womb-like baths, ruled over by Yohualticitl (Midwife of the Night)—an aspect of the Earth Mother Tonatzin (Our Holy Mother)—have changed little since the Spanish conquest. This is not through efforts to preserve tradition, but because some native tribes throughout southern Mexico and in Guatemala do not yet have modern amenities such as bathtubs and showers and still use original indigenous baths. In some villages of Mexico every backyard has a temezcal for family use.

111

Opposite: Statue of an Aztec water Goddess.

For the ancient Aztecs, the temezcal was a spiritual experience that included fasting, medicine songs, prayers, and chants designed to unblock creativity, distract the mind from obsessive thoughts, liberate the emotions, and enhance communion with ancestors and gods. Many of the prayers and chants for the sweat bath have been lost and many native people now see it as a place mainly for physical purification. There is, however, a resurgence of interest in its spiritual aspects.

Water and Aztec Creation

Like other Mesoamerican peoples, the Aztec believed it took several "creations," or Suns, before the gods got life right. Tlaloc ruled the Third Sun, which ended in a rain of fire. The Fourth Sun was ruled by Chalchiuhtlicue but was destroyed by a deluge. The force of this flood caused the sky to fall down, so the principal gods—Tezcatlipoca and Quetzalcóatl—made themselves into great trees and raised it back into place. Finally, the gods gathered at Teotihuacán to create a new Sun, our current world.

Building a Temezcal

Mexicans construct a temezcal using anything from adobe blocks to tent canvas slung over bent poles. Their temezcals can be as large as twenty feet in diameter and can be round or rectangular, but usually end up egg-shaped. Like those of their neighbors to the north and south, the fire pit is sunken into the earth. The floor can be covered with woven mats or banana leaves, and the entrance, with ceremonially gathered pine leaves, which stay in place between sweats.

Blessing a New Temezcal

Traditionally, a newly built *temezcal* must be blessed by a spiritual healer before it is used. This keeps out evil spirits, who love dark, moist, hidden "inside" places. When blessed and prepared properly, the *temezcal* has a great and powerful energy force. Improperly initiated, it can harbor evil spirits or dark energies that negatively affect the physical and spiritual health of those who come for healing.

In certain regions, a chicken is killed as a sacrificial offering before the temezcal is used. Offerings can also be as simple as a bottle of soda, holy water from the Catholic church, or rum. Candles dedicated to the gods of the sky and the earth are burned and chanted over. Copal incense may be used to ward off any evil influences and to ensure that the benevolent spirits will be present to guard over all participants and answer their pleas for healing and purification.

The Sweat

As in Native American sweat lodges, the stones are collected and heated in the pit seven at a time. An herbal tea made from eucalyptus, artemisia, rosemary, marigold, or basil is prepared to throw on the stones to create the fragrant steam.

Once participants have crawled inside, prayers and incantations are directed to the deities of the sun, moon, earth, and water and to the four directions. Sometime during the rounds of the sweat, a handful of seeds may be passed around. Each person prays for something they are seeking as they hold the seeds.

The Temazclera

The *temazcalera* or *temezclero* has the job of putting people at ease and creating a peaceful bathing environment. She or he manipulates the heat with branches of herbs. Sometimes bathers are smacked with the herbs or cornhusks to encourage circulation in specific areas of the body. After the sweat, some *temzecleras* sprinkle bathers with cool, fresh rainwater mixed with basil leaves to close the pores, then administer an herbal tea or vegetable or chicken broth. Some *temazcaleras* are also traditional healers or massage therapists.

New Mother Ritual

The most common use of the *temezcal* today is for women who have given birth within seven to twenty-one days. These post-partum baths provide both physical and spiritual cleansing: There is a belief that mothers in childbirth are exposed to many spirits, some good and some evil.

Traditionally, the mother is well wrapped and carried from her home to the *temezcal* on her husband's back or, more recently, on a board carried by two men. Younger women may walk, accompanied by their midwife or their grandmothers.

The baby is briefly exposed to the steam, then removed into the care of a relative. Then, a bunch of sapote (*achras zapota*) leaves is placed between the mother's thighs to cover the genitals. The midwife washes the mother's body with a piece of loofah sponge and soapy water. After thirty minutes or so, the mother is dried, wrapped tightly in warm covers, and carried out to rest. The other women of the family then crawl into the temezcal to pray for the well-being of both mother and child.

Midwives recommend four such post-partum baths for mothers, one every eight days.

A Full-Moon Bath from the Aztecs

The full moon is a time to bring projects and relationships to final fruition, so this ritual is suited to situations of that sort. Aztecs have always dearly loved their marigolds—*zempasuchitl* in the Aztec Nahuatl language, *flor de muerto* (flower of the dead) in Spanish—because of its ritual use on the Day of the Dead, November 1, when the deceased are honored. Any type of marigold will do for this bath except the pot marigold known as calendula; for this bath you need the highly aromatic garden variety of marigold. At noontime during the full moon phase, collect a quart of fresh marigold flowers. As you collect the flowers, concentrate on what you would like have come to full realization or closure and say the prayers. Empty the marigolds into a container with two gallons of water and allow them to soak in the sun for three hours, undisturbed. In the late afternoon before the sun sets, sit outside if it is warm enough. In small amounts, pour the flowers and the water over your head and body. If it feels too cold to you, add some heated water from the stove. When finished, let yourself air-dry if at all possible and contemplate the matter at hand.

Aztec Baptism: Baby Bathing and Naming Ritual

Four days after birth, the Aztecs bathed and named the child. To a boy they would give an infant-sized shield, cloak, bow, and four arrows; to a girl they would give a *huipil* and *cueitl* (blouse and skirt) and sewing implements. You can replace these with clothes and items you feel are symbolically appropriate to your child and his or her future.

At sunrise, place the clothes and items near a washbasin full of water. Scoop the water in your right hand, sprinkle the baby's, and say:

> "Take hold of this water, which will protect your life in the name of the goddess Chalchiuhtlicue."

Sprinkle the water on the baby's chest and say:

> "Receive this heavenly water, which washes the impurity from your heart."

Pour the water on the baby's head and say:

> "Child, receive the divine water—which if not drunk, nobody can live—so that it can cleanse you and eliminate your misfortunes, which form part of your existence since the beginning of the world. It is truly its peculiar property to oppose all adverse fortune."

Wash the baby completely and proclaim:

> "Which part of you hides unhappiness? In which member are you hidden? Leave the child. Today he/she is truly reborn through healthful waters with which he has been sprinkled under the guidance of the goddess of the sea. Provide this child with happiness throughout his/her life."

The Inca

Enhancing the Spiritual Power of Water

The ancient Inca believed that the cosmos consisted of invisible energy, or *kausay,* that permeates everything with a spiritual force known as *sami.* Inca priests and priestesses could see *sami* as a *poq'pos* or "bubble" of living, pulsating energy surrounding every physical body. Water, a carrier of energy, had the power to transform the energy around humans from dark and heavy to light-filled and refined.

The Inca were masters at enhancing the already powerful energies of water. They built stone cisterns to collect melting glacial ice that they believed flowed from the dwelling place of mountain gods, and they constructed their temples along the paths of sacred rivers. They manipulated the flow of water through elaborately tiered systems of stone channels and baths so that the water's spiritual energy could be stored and carried along from temple to temple, uniting them all within the sacred "bubble."

Praying over Water at Machu Picchu

Incan priests and priestesses sat in stone seats built alongside the water channels and intentionally merged their energies with the apu or spirits of the water. As the water cascaded from one stone bath to another, it gathered spiritual energy from the priests, the earth, the sun, and moon. Sometimes the priests and priestesses immersed themselves in a stone circle with niches or huaca carved into the wall in which golden idols were kept. After being blessed by the priests, the idols were placed above the channel so that their energy could also flow into the water.

117

Charged with the energies of nature and priests, the water entered a series of fountains within the temple. It was used for ritual baths and the initiation of high-ranking priests and priestesses. It was also sanctified for villagers to use for drinking, bathing, irrigation, and other domestic purposes. As a result, the villagers, plants, and animals all were blessed with the *sami* energies blended by the priests from the *apu* of the water, sun, moon, rocks, and mountains.

Machu Picchu, Tambomachay, and Other Incan Baths

In Machu Picchu—the sacred fortress city high in the Andes of northern Peru, where only those initiated into the sacred mysteries could enter or live—sparkling water cascades down steps, over rocks, and into pools, then runs under long expanses of masonry to re-emerge as fountains or waterfalls. The palaces and temples in the noble quarter feature a main bath precinct.

One of the temple complexes has seven levels of ritual baths; here water was imbued with spiritual forces and prayers. The highest, most advanced priest sat alone in the uppermost bath. Two priests, a man and a woman (representing the masculine and feminine polarities), sat in the sixth level, and one in the fifth. On each of the two lower levels sat a priest and priestess, symbolizing the confluence of feminine and masculine energies.

At the archaeological site of Tambomachay, not far from Machu Picchu, is "The Bath of the Inca." Here water still flows from the original aqueduct into a holding tank. Other famous baths near Machu Picchu are at the sacred sites of Winay Wayna, which translates as "ever young"; Phuyupatamarca; and Tipon.

Opposite: The Inca Royal Baths in Tambomachay, Peru.

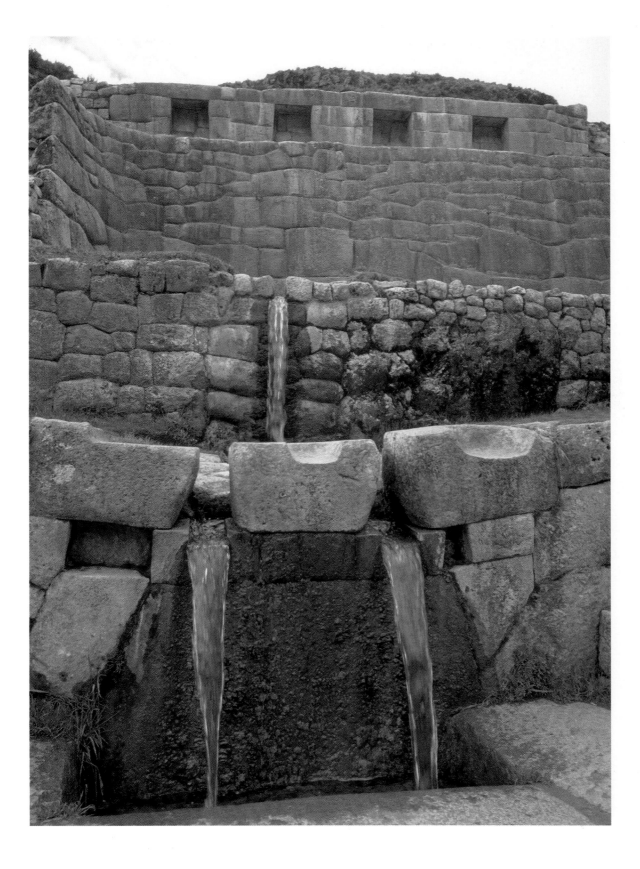

Rivers: Transporters of Spiritual Energy

Rivers, in particular, were powerful carriers of spiritual forces. It was believed that the *apu* or spirit of rivers expected to be honored with prayers and offerings known as *despachos*. The *despachos* given to river *apu* were said to be carried along the current from one temple site to another, delivering the prayers, requests, and gifts of the people to the gods and goddesses. River water was considered to have medicinal powers and was used by the shamans for healing purposes through prayer, invocation, and ritual baths.

The Urubamba River

Peru's most sacred river is the Urubamba, known also as the Vilcanota or Willkamayu in its upper reaches. The Urubamba was perceived as a strip of living feminine energy coursing along and within the earth like a moving snake. Inca shamans said that they could see a rainbow-colored spiritual bubble flowing along and above the Urubamba that was carried everywhere it flows. The river, they said, stretched out her energy force to embrace and empower each temple along her route. Bathers who immersed themselves in this sacred field of primal goddess energy merged with this force and released their heavy, dark energies into her waters. Incan legend said that the river was able to absorb, remember, and make human wishes come true if they are wished while bathing within her sacred bubble.

The Urubamba River and Sacred Valley, Peru.

Lake Titicaca

Lake Titicaca is Peru's largest lake and one of the world's highest navigable lakes. It is considered to be the birthplace of the Inca and the place of return for their ancestral spirits. Inca and Tihuanaco people have inhabited this area since as early as 1300 B.C.. The lake is also a sacred water site to the Aymara Indians, who live on its shore and still perform water rituals and ceremonies there.

According to an ancient myth, the islands of the sun and the moon in Lake Titicaca trembled when life was born. The Island of the Sun is the birthplace of Manco Capac and Mama Oqlla, the first Inca king and queen. On the Island of the Moon, the women danced and sang in the ancient Women's Temple. In the Temple of the Sun, under the watchful eyes of the guardian spirit Apu Illimani, the men participated in a ceremony honoring the sacredness of all life.

Aqua de Florida Baths

During the sacred Ayauasca ceremony, contemporary shamans and seekers alike ingest hallucinogenic plants to engender waking visions of spirit forces. Before participants drink the bitter herbal brew—ritually prepared in the forest by shamans—they are bathed with *agua de florida,* an aromatic, jade-colored mixture of various flowers. The *ayauasceros,* or shamans, ritually gather certain flowers with a prayer that is both a request for protection from evil spirits during the sacred journey and an invitation to good spirits to teach participants something vital to their physical and spiritual lives. The flowers are crushed into the water and set out to absorb the energy of the sun and the wind. This ablution—accompanied by prayer, chanting, or singing—is repeated the morning after the completion of the ceremony.

Hot Springs and Caves

Hot springs and caves were sites of pilgrimage and ceremony. Where hot springs gush from the center of the Pachamama or Earth Mother, the *apu* of water, earth, and fire combine to create a particularly powerful triumvirate. The Inca saw caves and their moist, dripping interiors—the source of rivers and lakes—as the womb of the earth that sends forth creation. The entrance to the cave is honored as the vagina of the Earth Mother, and the walls of the cave as the uterine flow that delivers life-giving fluids. The hot springs and caves all possessed high amounts of *kausay,* the invisible energy of the *apu.*

The Festival of the Sun

The largest and most famous Andean ritual is the Inti-raymi or Festival of the Sun on June 24. Thousands of Peruvians still visit the sacred sites to take a *bano sagrado,* the sacred bath, as part of a purification ceremony.

A Flower Bath at Home

The simple and powerful traditions of the Inca can easily be adapted to spiritual bathing at home or in the countryside. At home you can create a florecida by gathering whatever non-toxic and unsprayed flowers you might find in your backyard, or in the countryside if you are well-versed in identification of wild flowers. Some suggestions for wildflowers are St. John's wort, plantain, chicory, burdock, and yellow dock. Cultivated flowers you can use might include roses, zinnias, or marigolds, as well as leaves and flowers of peppermint, sage, thyme, rosemary, or basil.

To maximize their aromas and healing qualities you'll want to gather the flowers on a bright, sunny day between 11 a.m. and 4 p.m. Place a handful of flowers—either from a mixture of flowers or a single type of flower—in a basin, tub, or bucket that holds at least three to five gallons of water. Gently squeeze the flowers between your hands for a few minutes while saying prayers appropriate to your faith. Allow the flower-infused water to sit in the sun for a few hours. If the weather is warm enough, pour the water over yourself while sitting outside in the garden and allow yourself to air dry. Or you bathe in the shower while sitting on a wooden stool. Be sure to place a protective screen over the drain to avoid clogging the plumbing.

A Flower Bath in Peru

I was a member of the teaching staff at Explorama Lodge on the Amazon, about five hours by wooden dugout canoe from Iquitos, Peru. At the Pharmacy from the Rainforest, a week-long seminar attended by pharmacists, scientists, medical doctors, and a sprinkling of natural therapists, I taught a class on the role of women in shamanism in Central America. A lovely and gracious traditional healer from Iquitos, Julia Riveras, attended several of my sessions, even though she could not understand much English. After each class we talked excitedly in Spanish, sharing stories and our personal histories with healing and shamanism. Julia offered to prepare *florecidas* or flower baths for each member of the faculty over a period of a few days.

She invited me to assist her in this process, which of course I was delighted to do. Each of the next few days she appeared clutching enormous bouquets of fresh flowers in her ample arms. In the morning she squeezed the flowers and their leaves into several buckets of water that were then set out in the sun. One by one, the instructors came to the teacher's hut for their most unusual treatment.

Each was led into the outdoor bathing area, no more than four walls of a cane-like bush material with the roof open to the sapphire-blue sky above. Julia prayed to her deity before each bath, then slowly and reverently poured the flowery water over each person. They entered the bath looking and feeling tired and drained of energy from

rounds of lecturing—each of us had taught the same class twice daily for five days. They emerged looking and smelling refreshed and renewed. In fact, we all commented on what seemed to be beams of light emanating from around our bodies as we emerged from the spiritual bath.

Julia whispered her Inca prayers all the while as she poured the water over our strained heads and tired bodies. When it was finally my turn, I sat like an expectant child and allowed the rich, green, divinely aromatic water to be poured over me. The sunlight above warmed me and the water cooled me at the same time.

Several of us sat around the common area wearing only our bathing suits and allowed the flower petals to stay on us as long as possible. The eminent late Dr. Varro Tyler wore yellow marigold and red zinnia in his hair; Chinese acupuncturist and herbalist Michael Tierra had cascades of flowers up and down his abdomen and clinging to his eyelashes. Ethnobotanist Mark Plotkin could be heard giggling and making sounds of delight as he got his bath. We were no longer professors, but elves and fairies partaking in a sacred bathing ceremony. I felt lightened and exhilarated in body and soul. We laughed and cavorted like kids just let out of the confines of school. We all seemed happier and easier to be with for several days after the florecidas and Julia's ministrations.

—RA

The Hindus

Rivers of the Goddess

Hinduism itself is like a great streaming river, fluid and ever-evolving, with the ability to split itself, change direction, and be many paradoxical things at once. Nonjudgmental, it is content to live with its own contradictions, embrace rivals, and even take in entire religions (such as Buddhism), much as a river effortlessly divides and absorbs its tributaries. Its pantheon is dominated by Shiva, Vishnu, Brahma, and the Great Goddess, Devi. The Divine is also manifested in thousands of other divine beings, including Krishna, Ganesh, and Rama. The ultimate goal of Hinduism is simple: union with God—known as *yoga*—and an end to the feeling of separateness from God.

"Wash away, Waters, whatever sin is in me, what wrong I have done, what imprecation I have uttered, and what untruth I have spoken."

—RIG VEDA 10.9.8-9

Hindu philosophy proposes that the flow of human thought is or should be like a river, flowing from a higher to a lower plane. Every time the mind makes an effort to go within, back to its source, it is a moment of meditation. In that attempt are all creative beginnings made. Rivers are bridges between heaven and earth, the human and the divine.

Since at least as early as 1400 B.C., when the first of the sacred hymns of knowledge known as the Vedas—the Rig Veda—was composed, the Hindus have thought of water as energy in liquid form. Hindu sages linked the mysterious event of the Creation with water, conceiving of life as having developed from its primordial soup.

The Goddess Ganga Seated on Her Fish in a Landscape of Mountains and Trees, opaque watercolor and gold on paper, ca. 1815, India, Panjab Hills, Mandi, 11 3/16 x 8 15/32 inches. San Diego Museum of Art (Edwin Binney 3rd Collection).

Like the Inca, the Egyptians, the Kabbalists, and others, the Hindus view rivers as vessels for sacred and cleansing spiritual energy. Three great rivers of the Indian subcontinent—the all-powerful Ganges; the Yamuna, which flows out from the Himalayas past Krishna's birthplace at Mathura; and Saraswati, the eternal, mythical river of knowledge that is said to have disappeared from the earth and to have gone underground—and a host of other waters are personified as deities and honored for their life-giving qualities. In all, India has seven sacred rivers, often called the Seven Gangas, that supply its vast lands with sacred waters.

The Spiritual Origin of Rivers and the Nectar of Immortality

According to Hindu legend, after a long period of strife the gods and the demons agreed to put aside their differences and combine efforts, to churn the ocean and draw out the nectar of immortality and omnipotence—*amrita*—from the bottom of the oceans. They agreed to share it when they found it.

The gods and demons stood on opposite sides of the ocean and started churning the waters, using Seshnaga, the celestial cobra, as a paddle. The demons held the head of the serpent and the gods held the tail. The churning went on and on, and many divine gifts issued forth from the ocean: a holy cow; the flying horse; the lyre; Lakshmi, goddess of prosperity; and Vishvakarma, the divine architect and constructor. All these wonders were distributed equally between the gods and demons.

Last came Dhanavantri, the divine physician, bearing the coveted pitcher of amrita. The demons snatched it from him and ran away, leaving the gods behind with no nectar.

The gods then prayed to Lord Vishnu to retrieve their share from the demons. To deceive the demons, Vishnu took the form of an enchanting maiden, Mohini. Mohini approached the demons as they loudly argued about how to distribute the stolen nectar amongst themselves. Taking advantage of this confusion, Mohini offered to distribute the nectar, on the condition that it also be shared among the gods.

Under the captivating influence of Mohini, the demons agreed and she went about distributing the nectar. She arranged the gods and demons in rows so that the gods would be served first and there would be none left for the demons. In their rush, the gods spilled some of the nectar. It landed on the earth and became the sacred rivers.[1]

"....The people bathe in the Ganges. It's a constant baptism rite; going in and going out and absorbing the virtue of this miraculous gift of the universe, the waters of the Ganges...This flowing water is the grace that comes to us from the power of the female power."

—JOSEPH CAMPBELL

Lustration of a Jina, opaque watercolor on paper, ca. 1800–1825, India, Gujarat, 11 1/4 x 7 3/8 inches. Los Angeles County Museum of Art, gift of Leo S. Figiel, M.D.

The Ganges

The Ganges is known as *Ganga Mai*—Mother Ganges. She is both the personification of the goddess Ganga and the spiritual artery of India. Normally beneficent, in times of rain she may swell to life-threatening proportions.[2]

To a Hindu, the greatest goal is to be thrown into the Ganges after death or to have one's ashes spread on the body of the Mother so as to be reunited and in a state of complete oneness with her in spirit. This fulfills the ultimate objective, *moksha,* the forgiveness that brings liberation from the cycle of incarnation that is seen as a burden and a difficult passage.

Water from the Ganges purifies gods, people, and anything else with which it is combined; it is the spiritual elixir of the Hindus. Her liquid feminine energy absorbs spiritual pollution and carries it away. The waters of the Ganges are identified with the milk of mother cows and referred to as "mother" when being sipped by devout Hindus.

Devotees carry home Ganges water in jugs. The water is to be present at any priestly ritual and, ideally, at every *puja* or worship ceremony at home or in a temple. On such occasions, the water is sometimes held in a conch shell just like the shell that Devi holds in one of her many hands. At funerals, a little of the water is sprinkled on the body before cremation.

For those fortunate enough to bathe in her, the Ganges confers a divine blessing. There is also an element of forgiveness of sins or wrongdoing bestowed upon those who bathe in the Ganges.

The Kumbha Mela Festival

There are many occasions on which Hindus bathe for ritual purification in the Mother Ganges, but none is as impressive and popular as the massive pilgrimage to the Ganges, the North Indian Kumbh Mela festival. In Hindi, *kumbh mela* means "pot of nectar."

The Kumbh Mela can be traced back to river festivals in which pots of grains were soaked in the waters of the holy rivers and put to seed, with the rest of the grain, at sowing time. It was a pre-Aryan fertility ritual, for the *kumbh* symbolizes not only the mother goddess but also the womb. As givers of life and fertility, rivers became *tirthas*—holy places that are pilgrimage destinations—since they act as bridges between heaven and earth, the human and the divine.

The Kumbh Mela commemorates the moment when the gods wrested the nectar of immortality from the demons. One version of the legend has it that the gods were so exhilarated during their flight back to the Himalayan peaks that they accidentally spilt a few drops at four places: Ujjain, Nasik, Haridwar, and Allahabad. Every three years, a festival is held at one of these sites. The largest, every twelve years, is always at Allahabad, the sacred confluence of three holy rivers: the Ganges, the Yamuna, and the mythical Saraswati. Known as the Great Kumbh Mela or Purna Kumbh Mela, it represents complete *mela* or gathering because it is the completion of twelve lesser Kumbh Melas.

Tradition holds that the famous ninth-century sage, philosopher, and religious guru Shankaracharya organized the first festival, encouraging all the different monastic and philosophical schools to attend and exchange views. This came at a perfect time for Hinduism, which had recently been rocked by the breakaway religions of Buddhism and Jainism. The festival infused Hinduism with new life, quickly attracting many religiously inclined lay people. By the fourteenth century, records of the festival show that all its key modern elements were in place: the ritual bathing, the congregating of *sadhus* or ascetics, and the hordes of pilgrims.

Throughout the eras of Muslim and British domination, the Kumbh Mela helped preserve Hinduism. The modern festival still provides an occasion for Hindus of all schools to converge and celebrate the diversity of their religion. For most, it is a once-in-a-lifetime experience akin to the Muslim's pilgrimage to Mecca. Devout Hindus plan and save over many years to make this visit to the king of *tirthas*.

When they arrive, some with heads shaven, the pilgrims chant unceasingly *"Jai Ganga maiya"* ("Long live mother Ganga"). The highlight of the festival is the ritual bathing, for which the most auspicious hour is just before dawn at the time between the full moon and the new moons. Wearing the traditional loincloths and saris, and holding their palms together in the traditional style of Hindu prayer, the pilgrims dip themselves three times in the Ganges while reciting prayers and *"Jai Ganga maiya."*

With this ritual they renew their faith and cleanse their souls. Then they don fresh clothing and perform *puja* on the riverbank, en masse. After a meal, pilgrims may listen to the discourses of various *sadhus* having a *darshan* or meet with well-known sages who set up tents and sit cross-legged on mats to dispense their wisdom to the believers.

SWIMMING RITUALS

Devoted swimmers know that swimming is an ideal time for reflection, meditation, and finding clarity. There is a soothing calm that comes from within after the first few laps, be they in a pool or a natural body of water. This practice can be taken further, to conscious meditation and direct spiritual connection.

Deep breathing is one of the hallmarks of meditation. Combine this with the rhythmic motions, the powerful feeling of forward movement, the comfort and joy of being surrounded by water, and the sound of the water in the ears, and many swimmers achieve a trance-like state. If one is swimming outside, the sun and rain or clouds above add another dimension of nature appreciation.

Before each of the following meditations, it is best to first swim for about ten minutes to warm up or until you find the "zone" of regular breathing and movement.

Swimmer's Meditation

Try to empty your mind. Let the thoughts flow, gently acknowledging them as they arise and letting them go. Don't let any particular thought absorb you. Note it and let it go. Listen for the answers of your heart.

A Spiritual Swim

Feel the joy of swimming throughout every part of your body.
Acknowledge the joy of nature, above and below you.
Contemplate the blessing and the role of water in daily life.
Pay attention to your breath.
Let your breath be your prayer.
or
Compose a mantra in your head and say it to yourself over and over again.
Breathe out close to the surface water, if you can; feel and see the vibrations of your breath on the water.
Feel the energy of the water.
Imagine that you're surrounded by God or the Divine.
Feel embraced by the Divine: held, loved, warmed.

A Rose-Water Aspersion for Your Home

Aspersion means to bless by sprinkling water. Hindu temple attendants in India sprinkle rose water inside and outside of the temple before opening to the public and after closing. After there has been a shouting match, a period of tension or non-communication, or a traumatic event that upsets everyone, it is a good time to clear the air with this simple ritual.

You can purchase bottles of rose water at most stores that specialize in Middle Eastern foods, or make your own. Gather four red roses at noontime, when they are at their peak of bloom and the plant's vital energy is circulating above the ground. Place them in a basin of water in the sun or by a sunny window for a few hours.

First, put away papers and whatever else you don't want to get wet. Center yourself with some prayers or a meditation that is appropriate for you. Pour the rose water into a portable vessel. While keeping the intention of clearing out the bad feelings, sprinkle the entire house or any room with the rose water. With the vessel in one hand, dip palmfuls of water and sprinkle generously around each room, especially in each of the four corners. Continue until every room has been sprinkled. Keep your purpose and intent in mind the whole time. One appropriate statement is, "All sorrow and evil must now leave this place. I have faith with all my heart that this will be so." If you have a companion to follow behind you and burn incense, so much the better, or you can burn the incense before you start sprinkling.

One good sprinkling will make a major difference. You might want to repeat this as needed—especially if there is ongoing turmoil in the household—or at least once a month just for good measure.

Turmeric House Bathing Ritual

Hindus believe that turmeric can cool things down when the emotions and circumstance of our lives heat up. It can dispel powerful emotions from within a home and bring a calming glow into the family environment.

~ If using powdered turmeric, mix one tablespoon in one quart of water. Shake well and place where it will be undisturbed in the sun for one hour.

~ If using fresh turmeric, grate the tubers until you have three tablespoons. Pour boiling water over it and allow it to steep for thirty minutes.

~ Holding the vessel in one hand, dip the other hand in the water and sprinkle palm-fuls of water generously around each room, especially in the four corners. Continue until every room of the house is sprinkled.

The Buddhists

Bathing Others for the Next Reincarnation

For Buddhists, bathing others is a spiritual action that ensures good fortune in future lives. In the *Sutra on Baths and Bathing for the Clergy,* The Buddha has much advice for a monk who wishes to gain merit by bathing the Buddha and his disciples in a bath that he has prepared.

One of the seven benefits of spiritual baths, the Buddha explains, is that in every life into which you are reborn you will be lovely in form and pure in person.

"At birth you will be naturally clothed and adorned with everlastingly brilliant jewels. Indeed, those who are born into this world with pleasant features admired by others, and who are pure and clean and lustrous-skinned, are those who, in their former lives, provided baths for monks and have been thus rewarded. These rewards are also obtained as the result of providing baths for monks: birth as the son of a great minister and enjoyment of a wealth of treasures; birth in the house of a great king, where you are bathed with fragrant incense and perfumed water; protection in all four directions through the power of the Four Celestial Kings; enjoyment of a long life; and [the opportunity to] revel in the pleasures of the Six Desire Heavens to the utmost, and dwell in the perfect quiescent state in Brahma's Heaven."[1]

The Buddha then spoke of seven necessary objects for bathing: firewood; pure water; bean husks for scrubbing; bath oil to moisten, cool, and soften the body; finely ground ashes; willow-twig toothpicks; and bath robes. Bathing, he added, also had benefits for the current incarnation: relaxation of the body; avoidance of colds, pains, chills, fever, and filth; refreshing of the body; and clearing of vision.

Opposite: A torii gate stands in shallow water reflecting the sunlight, Hiroshima, Japan.

135

Japan: Bathing in the Memories of Water

Surrounded by the sea and blessed with fast-running streams and rivers and abundant hot water from mineral springs, the Japanese have always held water as a source of life and revered it as an object of worship. The ancient Japanese believed that water held the memory of the mountains on which it fell to earth, the rocks over which it bubbled in high mountain streams, the sun that warmed it, and eventually the earth that held it. Water carried these glorious memories with it as it flowed into the valleys and the streams and rivers. It shared them with the people of the valleys, who bathed in and drank the water.

Water, then, was purifying. From earliest times until the present day, Shintoism insisted on ritual and actual purity. Evil and immorality were associated with filth and pollution, and virtue and goodness with cleanliness and purity. Bathing in water cleansed the soul and was necessary in order to communicate with the gods.[2]

When Buddhism penetrated into Japan in the seventh century, it mingled effortlessly with Shinto beliefs, and even today the Shinto and the Buddhist practitioner live together harmoniously. Most Zen Buddhist temples and monasteries were built with bathing facilities where priests and monks could purify their minds and bodies and hold counsel. The baths were soon opened to pilgrims, who were bathed for free by priests and monks as way to acquire merit.[3] Water was heated in large cauldrons and drawn off by pipes or buckets to smaller wooden vats. The cauldrons were counted among the chief assets of a temple; during periods of rivalry between religious sects, they were often stolen from one temple and installed in another. In 1199, for example, monks from the Kofuku-ji temple in Nara raided Horyu-ji, steal-

The Birth of Buddhism

The Buddha, "the enlightened one," was born in fifth-century India as Gautama Siddhartha, but had had many other names in previous incarnations. Monks often say that Buddhism is more philosophy than religion, since its primary goal is to understand your own mind and its attachments and dissatisfactions in order to attain enlightenment. The Sanskrit root *budh* means to be awake and to know.

Buddhism spread from India throughout Asia, taking slightly different forms in each country. In the seventh century it spread from Korea to Japan, sparking the rise of Zen Buddhism—a blend of Buddhism, Shinto, and a loose coalescence of Japanese regional legends, ancestral myths, primitive forms of nature worship, and communal folk beliefs.

ing the tub from the temple bathhouse. Today the Japanese monasteries and temples still offer spiritual baths to pilgrims in continuation of the medieval custom.[4]

Although charity baths originated in China and Korea, they became particularly popular in Japan. Because purging other people's afflictions of body and soul was considered an act of great charity, it became a custom for the rich to bathe the poor and for hosts to bathe their guests. Wealthy patrons sponsored baths for the poor. Known as *seyoku,* this practice grew more widespread as Buddhism developed from a purely monastic religion to a popular faith with large congregations of lay worshipers. *Seyokum* could be arranged at a temple by donating money or large quantities of firewood or fuel for heating bath water. A single bath might be donated or arrangements could be made for charitable baths in perpetuity. In this way, wealthy believers might gain religious merit during their lifetimes and the repose of their souls after death.[5]

Empress Koyo, consort of Emperor Shomu, who lived during the eighth century, was made the patron saint of charity baths after her death. She had vowed to bathe one thousand beggars with her own hands in the bathhouse of the Hokke-ji temple at Nara. Legend relates that after scrubbing nine hundred and ninety-nine beggars, she looked up to see that the last was a leper—and the virtuous empress didn't flinch. The thousandth beggar revealed himself to her as the Buddha, who had come to aid her progress toward enlightenment.[6]

Waterfalls

It is fitting that waterfalls are one of the basic motifs of Asian landscape paintings. The dynamic downward movement of the water contrasts with both the upward movement of the rock and its static property, creating a yin-yang relationship between mountain and water. As both Zen Buddhists and the ancient Greek philosopher Heraclitus have observed, the same water never flows through the same river or over the same rocks, illustrating the impermanence of all life. Waterfalls are also symbols of infinite potential.

Understandably, then, the great, inspiring waterfalls hidden away in remote mountain areas have been places of adoration and pilgrimage since earliest history. To the Shinto, the waterfall is a *go-shintai* or symbolic physical embodiment of a *kami,* or god. Water *kami* are still worshipped at temples that dot the country, many of which are located at waterfalls.

Monks, priests, shamans and ascetics, and aspirants to the life of devotion have long bathed themselves at waterfalls, for spiritual purification before entering mountain shrines, and to replenish their healing and divining powers in the presence of

Coming Forth from the Bath

The major deities of the ancient Shinto cosmos—the gods of sun, moon, and fertility—were all born from the water of a bath in which Izanagi, the ultimate creator-ancestor, washed his body. In subsequent myths, the divine actors repeatedly immerse themselves in rivers or the sea and engage in all manner of ritual purifications. The sun and the moon themselves were revealed by the washing of Izanagi's eyes.[7]

the water god. They believed that bathing in the icy cold waters of the cascade heightened their spiritual powers, purified them from pollution, and prepared them for arduous tasks. Special inns developed, offering lodging to the mountain ascetics where they could be free to wander the slopes and valleys undisturbed. Gradually, the beliefs of the mountain cults and Buddhism merged into a belief system in which the nature spirits and *kamis* were considered aspects of the Buddha. "Mountains and waterfalls were now seen as geographical places attainable in time and space, at which were revealed the higher truths of the nonmaterial Absolute."[8]

Japan's most sacred waterfall is near Kumano, on the Kii Peninsula in Wakayama Prefecture on the Pacific Ocean. It is the shrine at Nachi, one of three sacred places there. The Nachi shrine arose out of the numinous beauty of the waterfall itself, which was considered to be a manifestation of the transcendent beauty of the Buddha. The god who watches over the cascade and represents the Buddha is known as Taki no Miya, also identified with Kannon (also known as Kuan Yin), the compassionate thousand-armed bodhisattva.

As explained in the Lotus Sutra, the most influential text in Japanese Buddhism, Kannon was deemed a bodhisattva of limitless compassion and had the ability to respond to everyone in need of salvation. Falling water is often used as a metaphor to describe salvation through Kannon. Her compassion is described as "pouring spiritual rain like nectar, quenching the flames of distress."

A group of mountain ascetics devoted to waterfalls was known as the Shugendo. The Shugendo ascetics came to immerse themselves in the freezing waters of the Nachi waterfall, even in the winter months. The most famous person to test his mettle at the waterfall was an ex-soldier, Mongaku Shonin (1160–1203) who became a monk and decided to test his religious commitment and fitness for his new calling by undergoing some severely austere self-imposed spiritual trials. He submitted his body to biting insects for seven days. Then, in the midst of winter, he vowed to stand under the waterfall at Nachi while invoking the sacred name of Fudo-Myoo three hundred thousand times. After five days, he fainted and was carried downstream by the current, from which he was rescued unconscious by a divine youth. Still, he returned to the icy waterfall for another three days before his strength again failed and he collapsed. This time two divine rescuers identified themselves as messengers of Fudo-Myoo, who had finally taken pity on Mongaku. After that, when he returned to the waterfall the freezing water felt warm and gentle on his body for the remainder of the prescribed twenty-one days. At the end, he was a holy priest.

The Benefits of Waterfall Baths

There may be some scientific underpinning for the feeling of renewal experienced by waterfall bathers. It is now believed that the negative ions said to be present in falling water transform our internal and external energy. The more water sprays, the more negative ions are purportedly created.[9] Scientists have found that burn victims exposed to negative ions require less skin grafting and less pain medication. Postoperative patients sleep and recover better when exposed to negative ions. In contrast, exposure to positive ions from generators and power lines may make people cranky and prone to rudeness, and it may slow the healing process.

Ions act on our ability to absorb oxygen. Negative ions in the bloodstream accelerate the delivery of oxygen to our cells and tissues, frequently giving a euphoric lift to the emotions. Positive ions depress the delivery of oxygen to the tissues, thereby retarding healing and increasing pain sensations.

Unfortunately, our air-conditioned, humidity-regulated modern buildings, buses, and planes become supercharged with harmful positive ions because the metal blowers, filters, and ducts strip the air of negative ions. Many modern-day Japanese believe these controlled indoor environments are intrinsically polluted.

Ancient Japanese Infant Washing

Elaborate washing rituals, comparable in significance to the baptismal rites of Christianity, followed the birth of any Japanese child. The rituals lavished on a child of imperial birth were of special splendor: An infant prince was ceremonially bathed twice daily by royal attendants.

Utensils and tubs used for the ritual bath were prepared with great care and purified waters were ceremonially drawn. All members of the highest ranks of the aristocracy were present in great finery. Elaborate meals were served, gifts presented, and poems and prayers recited.

Social Bathing

"There is, one realizes on careful reflection, no shortcut to moral learning like the public bath. It is after all the way of nature, and of heaven and earth, that all are naked when they bathe—the wise and the foolish, the crooked and the straight, the poor and the rich, the high and the low. The nakedness of infancy purges them all of sorrow and desire, and renders them selfless, be they Sakyamuni or Confucius, Gonsuke or Osan. Off with the wash water comes the grime of greed, and the passion of the flesh; a master and his servant are equally naked when they rinse themselves. As surely as an evening's red-faced drunkard is ashen and sober in the morning bath, the only thing separating the newborn baby's first bath from the cleansing of the corpse is life, fragile as a paper screen."

—SHIKITEI SAMBA, 1810[10]

During the seventh century, public bathhouses opened in Japan and became communal gathering places, especially for the working classes, who wanted a place where they could shed problems and connect with friends. Bathing became a social as well as a spiritual event. A Japanese proverb states, "Bathing buddies are the best of friends." Family ties were reinforced by sharing a tub and by scrubbing each other's backs. Men and women bathed together naked with no sense of shame—until the Americans came in after World War II, bringing their values with them.

The Japanese passion for bathing continues—it is the custom to bathe once or twice daily, in a natural body of water, a porch bath, or an elegant Japanese-style home bathroom. Most people bathe after returning home from work. But few modern Japanese consider their passion for immersing their bodies in the nearly scalding water to be an expression of spirituality. Nevertheless, bathing remains a communion with the values and the piety of their forebears.

Onsen

It is a popular pastime to visit seacoast, mountain, and countryside springs. These springs range from saline to sulphurous and from very hot to scalding hot. Resorts known as *onsen* have sprung up around these pools since ancient times. One well-known onsen is in the village of Dogo, on Shikoku Island, where steaming hot water gushes from the volcanic crevices under the ancient village. A 3,000-year-old legend relates that the hot spring was first discovered during the age of the Shinto gods, when a white heron healed its injured leg by immersing it in hot water gushing out of a rocky crevice.

Baptism of the Buddha Ritual

Each April 8, the statue of the baby Buddha standing in a bronze basin is taken out of its shrine and a ceremony of baptism with sweet tea made of vegetable leaves is performed. Afterward the tea is given away to children. This celebration takes place on a grand scale in all the larger cities of Japan; it is attended not only by Zen followers but by all Buddhists, including monks, and the general public of all ages.

Hotel Baths

Most good hotels in Japan now offer highly popular single-gender public baths. While still in their rooms, bathers are provided with a *yukata,* a casual cotton kimono that is totally acceptable garb for hotel hallways, gift shops, restaurants, and even the streets of Japan. The hot water of the public bath is meant for soaking, not for cleaning, so bathers must wash thoroughly before dipping into the hot baths; the Japanese are very serious about this rule. The hot bath is extremely hot, but still safe and very therapeutic.

Rotenburo

In outdoor pools known as *rotenburo,* bathers come close to a primal communion with nature. Rotenburo means "a bath amid the dew under an open sky." This definition captures the exquisitely lyrical sensation of this type of bath, in which, naked and immersed in clear hot water, one is exposed to the sky or stars overhead. There are hotels, resorts, magazines and even a television program devoted to the pleasures of rotenburo.

SPIRITUAL BATHING RITUALS

Clearing Ritual for the Healing Space or Home

Furniture, clothing, rugs, and draperies can absorb rays of energy as well as we can, so it is a good idea to freshen up the environment of your work space or home at least once a week—or even daily, if you are a practitioner who deals with many clients who express strong emotions. This is also a good way to cleanse a space that has just experienced a family argument or the presence of a negative visitor. It is also advisable to perform this clearing before moving into a new house or apartment.

You will need a spritzer bottle of the type used for misting houseplants. In the morning before going to work, or at any time, prepare a basin of fresh cool tap or spring water by crushing a white rose, a marigold, or the flowers and/or leaves of aromatic herbs such as oregano, basil, thyme, hyssop, or rosemary into one to two pints of water. Squeeze well and allow the mixture to sit for four to eight hours.

Strain and pour into the spritzer bottle. If possible, store in a refrigerator when not in use. If not refrigerated, the mixture will last only one day.

Spritz everything and everywhere in the house or room and ask that all negativity be released and removed from the space. It is a good idea to have a window or a door open to allow the flow of air that can carry away negative vibes. Use the spritzer on yourself, in your office, and over the chair or treatment table after sessions, too.

An alternative is to add two drops of your favorite essential oil to a one-pint spritzer bottle full of water. Lavender, rose, oregano, basil, rosemary, and neroli are all good choices.

Charity Baths

As a spiritual service you might consider offering a charity bath to someone in need of special nurturing. If you know someone who has suffered a traumatic experience you can offer to soothe his or her mind and emotions with one of the many baths in this book. A flower bath or one with essential oils, incense, and candles offered with love can be healing and give a sense of renewed hope and clarity. Even a simple foot bath in warm water goes a long way. Consider a gentle foot massage with rose or lavender oil.

A Friend's Ritual for Overcoming a Broken Heart

Ever wish you could really be helpful to someone who is experiencing a broken heart due to a romantic loss? This following ritual is guaranteed to give you "something to do" in the way of aid and sustenance. The lover may not return to her arms, but she will be better prepared to deal with the loss and more likely to accept the situation and see it as a stepping stone or an opportunity for spiritual growth.

Invite her over for tea or wine when you both have the time that this ritual will require. Tell her you have something special planned just for her that will make her feel much better afterward. A few hours before she is to arrive, prepare your bathroom as if for a sacred event—because that's what it is. You will need several candles, incense, fresh, fluffy towels, a bathrobe, a floor mat, and some light, dreamy music. If it is summertime, pick nine white roses or nine marigold flowers (either will do) that have not been sprayed with toxic chemicals. While picking these, clearly and firmly state the intention that you ask these flowers to wash away your friend's pain and grief. Give thanks for their assistance and state your faith as if it were already done.

Place the flowers in a basin of water in the sun. If it is winter, or if you just can't get the flowers, you can use essential oil of rose. In that case, add the oil when the bath is ready.

Incense is very important to help dispel the emotions of sadness and grief. Ideally, use copal resin, or dried rosemary, sage, or cedar burned over easily available briquettes made especially for that purpose. If you can't find any of these incenses, burn a stick of sandalwood.

If you offer wine, be sure that neither of you gets drunk; pour one glass apiece and just sip. Listen to her, allowing ample time for her to unload her worst fears and hurts. Then, when you feel the time is right, lead her to the bathroom, light the candles, turn on the music, and fill the tub with comfortably warm water. Just before she is ready to get in, pour in the flowers and water from the basin or add nine drops of essential oil of rose. Sit by her side, wipe her tears, hand her tissue, and get her what-ever she needs to be comfortable. Dip a wooden bowl into the bath water and pour its contents over her head, neck, and shoulders nine times, saying prayers out loud, asking that this grief, pain, and loss be washed away. The Lord's Prayer or any prayer appropriate to the faith of either of you is fine. When in doubt, "Thy will be done" always works.

Give her some time to be alone. When she is ready, receive her with a warm towel and help her to dry off and get dressed. You'll both be amazed at how relieved and renewed she will feel. Finish the evening in the way that suits you best; perhaps a funny video or sharing stories of overcoming adversity.

Bath for a Woman in Labor

It is very soothing for a woman in labor to sit in a tub of nicely warmed water while her husband or midwife pours water over her belly. The bath water can be enhanced by adding motherwort, St. John's wort, or marigold, all wonderful healing plants for mothers. Obviously this situation requires the utmost caution: be careful she does not slip and fall. Ideally, each bath can last for about twenty minutes. They can be given as often as the mother requests and the birth attendant feels appropriate.

Post-Partum Bath for Mother

After the baby is born, when the mother is feeling back to normal, treat the mother to a warm *(not hot)* herbal bath or a sponge bath. The best choices for this are moth-erwort, plantain, comfrey, and marigold. You can choose one of these or combine them in any way that appeals to you. Follow the general instructions for preparing baths (see page 167), using either fresh or dried plants. Help the mother gently into the tub; the water level should be about up to her chest. Put a pillow behind her head if possible and let her soak in quiet for twenty minutes. If you are giving a sponge bath, be sure she is in a comfortable position. This is a good time to burn candles and incense.

Turmeric House Bathing Ritual

Hindus believe that turmeric can cool things down when the emotions and circumstance of our lives heat up. It can dispel powerful emotions from within a home and bring a calming glow into the family environment.

~ If using powdered turmeric, mix one tablespoon in one quart of water. Shake well and place where it will be undisturbed in the sun for one hour.

~ If using fresh turmeric, grate the tubers until you have three tablespoons. Pour boiling water over it and allow it to steep for thirty minutes.

~ Holding the vessel in one hand, dip the other hand in the water and sprinkle palm-fuls of water generously around each room, especially in the four corners. Continue until every room of the house is sprinkled.

The Thais, Cambodians, and Chinese

Splashing with the Gods

The rivers and streams that crisscrossed old Siam blessed it with fertility, creating a close, respectful relationship between water, land, and people. *Mae nam* or "mother water" is the Thai expression for river and the Thai people greatly revere rivers as the source of goodness and life.

When Buddhism arrived, it absorbed indigenous Thai customs, and water came to symbolize the purity of the teachings of the Buddha. Its bright, transparent surface was a divine representation of compassion and virtue that washed away sins. Even today, Thai Buddhists liken mental clarity and a fresh, lucid mind to the sight of an unpolluted canal.[1]

Thai temples and shrines were built facing rivers because the Buddha achieved enlightenment as he sat under a bodhi tree facing a river. Where no rivers flow, a statue of a *naga*—a mythical being, half-human and half-serpent, which can appear in either guise and is associated with water—adorns the entrances to temples as a symbolic replacement.[2]

147

The Songkran Festival

Thais believe that the act of tossing water on everyone and everything appeases the ancestral spirits and brings good fortune and health to the community. A three-day festival of water sprinkling and splashing known as Songkran (meaning "movement" or "the passing of") commemorates the Thai New Year, which falls in April when the sun passes from the sign of Aries to the sign of Taurus. Songkran falls at the end of the farmers' harvest season, when the weather is sweltering, so the energetic splashing is a welcome reprieve from the heat and hard work. The splashing represents the purification of the soul and a new beginning for the new year. During the festival, offerings of water and food are made to the spirits of mountains, rivers, and streams.

The Three Days of Songkran

The holiday is celebrated on the last day of the old year and the first day of the new year. Festivities commence when villagers gather together early in the morning to bring offerings of food to the local monks. Then participants return home to bathe their Buddha images, thoroughly clean the house inside and out, and sprinkle scented water throughout the entire compound and on every family member. Even pets are sprinkled.

Later in the day, villagers perform the rite of *song nam* by bathing monks and images of the Buddha while praying for blessings and answers to prayers in the coming year. The sacred image of the Buddha is carried from the temple and placed in the outer courtyard. Celebrants in full ceremonial dress line up, carrying bowls of scented water to sprinkle on the Buddha image.

Meanwhile, the monks, dressed in their saffron robes, sit in a small shelter that has been erected for the occasion. Villagers, who are not allowed to enter the shelter, pour copious in amounts of scented water through three bamboo pipes, drenching the monks.

This monk-drenching ritual has its roots in the belief that this is the day that the Buddha comes down from heaven to bless the people. The monks act as channels or conduits for this sacred event; they must not be touched by the villagers.

After the ritual bathing of the monks, young people of both genders bend down so that the monks—still attired in their soaking-wet robes—can walk on their backs in a long line extending from the bath shelter to the temple. This commemorates the Buddha's return to heaven after he descended to bestow his divine blessing on the people and the land. "We act as the ladder that helps the Buddha get back," explains one celebrant.

Songkran is also a time of atonement for the wrongdoings of the previous year, and a moment to look to both the past and the future. Younger people listen respectfully to the problems and hardships of relatives in the past year, and to news of future marriages, births, and community events. Sons and daughters pour scented water over the hands of parents and grandparents to ask forgiveness if they have caused them worry or distress in the past year.

The elders then show forgiveness to their offspring by blessing them with a sprinkling of water. In some more traditional homes, the elders are bathed in the morning and given a new set of clothing with which to greet the new year.

Participants gain merit over the three days of the festival by rescuing fish out of rivers before the dry season starts and releasing them when the rivers swell again; releasing caged animals into the wild; and carrying new sand into the temple and helping with repairs. Everyone is careful not to commit bad deeds or entertain evil thoughts, which could have dire consequences in the new year.

On the last day of the festival, young people are blessed in the temple. A parade of celebrants playing traditional musical instruments bestows their good wishes for happiness and contentment in life on the youngsters. After this blessing, the parade leaves the temple for the homes of the village elders.

Then the communal splashing continues with total and complete abandon. Revelers are invited to come back down to earth, as the Buddha did, by splashing each other with scented water from traditional bowls. In larger towns, buckets of lustral water are placed along every street corner and passers-by are drenched with blessings of water. Even trucks are called into spiritual service; they are driven up and down the highways to supply the towns and villages with water to splash on each other, strangers, monks, and Buddha statues. The celebration gets raucous but everyone has fun and collects blessings as well. Songkran is an appropriate and traditional time for flirtation and romance, and some lucky young people find a bride or groom in the midst of all the merriment.

Cambodian Spirit Boats Ritual

For the Khmer, water's life energy is guarded over by the mythical naga. The naga takes many forms in Asian cultures; in Cambodia, it's often depicted as a hooded serpent who lives in underwater kingdoms in magnificent palaces studded with gems and pearls. The nagas are highly venerated in Cambodia, a reflection of earlier customs venerating land and water spirits. Its image adorns many of the balustrades at temples; it is said to link the human and the divine world.

An old but still-active custom among the Cambodians is the "spirit boat." Made out of paper, it has straw figures seated inside representing the boatman and passengers. The spirit boat is set in the rice fields so that when the floods come the boat will float out to the waters of the lake to carry the hopeful prayer and wish of the boat's maker to the spirits.[3]

Traditional Water Rituals

Wedding Ritual

On their wedding day, a couple sits together as guests pour holy water from conch shells into their joined hands. Sometimes they are doused with buckets of water and experience their first embrace as they attempt to escape the drenching.

Ritual for the Unquiet Mind

Monks sprinkle holy water on gathering crowds; the cool drizzle is intended to calm the moral chaos plaguing individual minds.

Rite of Passage for Five-year-old Boys

When young boys around the age of five have their topknots shaved off for the first time, they are ritually bathed to signify this as a rite of passage from childhood to adolescence.

Ritual for the Recently Deceased

When someone dies, the body is ceremonially bathed by a close family relative, usually an adult child. For each friend or relative who arrives at the funeral, a drop of water is dripped into the hands of the deceased to ensure that his or her next abode will be pure and clear.

Ritual for the Deceased

To help the deceased have a peaceful afterlife, good deeds are dedicated to them. This intention is announced by pouring water on the earth while gazing fixedly at the liquid as it leaves the glass, falls through the air, and touches the earth. This custom also requires the living to think about the purity of their intentions in making this sacrifice.

China: The Virtue of Water

Wen Tzu wrote that water by its very nature tends to purity; Lao Tse taught that water is the emblem of the highest virtue. The highest form of goodness is like water, he said, for the virtue of water is that it comes to the aid of ten thousand people without talk. Water is also a Taoist symbol of wisdom.[4] Water—yin—corresponds to the north, cold, the winter solstice, the kidneys, and the trigram K'an, the abyssal. Nevertheless, Chinese alchemists often thought of water as fire and ablutions could be thought of as cleansing by fire.

The Africans

Balancing Inner and Outer Worlds

Long before Christianity and Islam came to Africa, the continent was home to a plethora of indigenous religions and water cults. Even now, there are as many different religions in Africa as there are ethnic language groups, but most have a common belief in one supreme God, lesser gods of nature, and ancestor spirits. Water is generally perceived as a living substance that can, through ritual, help alleviate the misfortunes and problems of human life.

Rituals are crucial to indigenous African cultures; they harmoniously align the human world with the world of the gods, ancestors, and nature, and create balance between human inner and outer worlds. Some tribes and communities were fortunate enough to hold onto their traditions during the colonial era; others, under the watchful eyes of zealous missionaries, managed to continue the annual cycle of ritual by blending their own customs with those of western religion. Today many Africans are rediscovering their rich spiritual bathing traditions.

"The spirit of water is the spirit that watches over the fetus as it develops, promising it a home and the prosperity it needs to fulfill its purpose after it is born."
—MALIDOMA PATRICE SOMÉ

Opposite: A Bantu Christian is baptised in a river.

West Africa

The Dagara people of Africa live in what is now Burkina Faso (formerly Upper Volta), a small West African nation surrounded by Benin, Côte d'Ivoire, Ghana, Mali, Niger, and Togo. As a child, Malidoma Patrice Somé, contemporary Dagara shaman and writer, was taken away from his village and given a western education by Catholic missionaries. Later, he returned to his village to learn the ways of his people, and he now teaches westerners about African cultural traditions.

"Life, as Dagara people say, began underwater," says Somé. "Thus every form on the earth got its life signature in the waters and continues to live intimately with water." Water is crucial to the spiritual journey in that it allows Africans to maintain the kind of consciousness that links them to the Other World—that of ancestral and nonancestral spirits.

According to the Dagara, the earth is a child of Water, since the earth didn't exist until Water appeared. It was Water that cooled the fire of the cosmos and firmed the fiery earth so that it could give and support life. Thus, to the indigenous African, challenges, obstacles, chaos, and confusion in daily life are symbolic of a rise in fire. When a person grieves or is angry or afraid, he or she returns to fire—and only water can cool, quiet, and reconcile the burning psyche. Even physical illness is portrayed as a fire that pushes a person's energy beyond what he or she can handle.

Water "bestows serenity upon a person in turmoil," explains Somé. "Water seeks to cleanse, reconcile, and balance that which is in agitation, emotional disorder, and self-anger."[1] African healing wisdom also dictates that even those who are not ill need water to stay balanced, oriented, and reconciled.

According to Somé, Dagara water rituals are "attempts to unite things that must be united, to reconcile things that are meant to be together in the interest of the community. Water rituals tie up loose ends that are obstacles to our balance and reconciliation, our peace and serenity."[2]

Rites of passage—such as birth, puberty, marriage, and death—are also times of change that harken back to the chaos of creation; thus these times are marked and aided by ritual baths. One kind of ritual, full immersion in cold water, is considered a radical measure aimed at producing massive cathartic results, and a new beginning for the recipient.

Dagara Water Rituals

Annual Reconciliation Ritual

This cleansing ritual is one that needs to be done often because of the very human need to be cleansed of negative energy regularly. Although missionaries tried unsuccessfully to suppress it, whole villages continue to gather for this reconciliation ritual at the local river.

In the water, healers await villagers who come for healing. As the villager approaches the water, he or she is received by the healers and reminded of the spiritual depth of the event. The villager then enters the water and walks to the main healer, who asks a series of questions:

~ Do you understand the meaning of cleansing?

~ Do you admit to being in need of it?

~ Do you acknowledge that this cleansing can only be granted by the ancestors?

The healer reminds the villager that he or she is not the one who is doing the healing, but that it is a gift from the spirit who dwells in the water. The healer then dunks the villager in the water and keeps the head underwater for as long as the breath can be held—sometimes, even a little bit beyond—to ensure a breakthrough. According to tradition, the water spirit does not come until the supplicant is very uncomfortable.

Community Grieving Ritual

In indigenous Africa, human emotions are seen through the lens of the community and are sacred. As a result, individual healing is a village effort. In the case of personal loss, a group gathers together to help a person express grief and to show the person that their loss is a loss for the entire community. They hear about the loss and affirm how much this person means to the community. They grieve spontaneously and collectively. In many cases, tears and a powerful display and discharge of emotions are involved. The public nature of this catharsis—the visibility and recognition—washes away self-doubt. The success of this ritual depends on the undisturbed, focused attention of the community. When the crowd is large, it forms into an egg shape, symbolizing water, with the village on one side and the shrine on the other. The grieving ritual usually takes three days. At the end of the ritual they wash themselves in a natural place of cold running water, allowing the flow to carry away the last remnants of their grief and bringing "reconciliation and the return of balance." Somé observes, "When the emotional stream is released, it has to drip itself to dryness before it is stopped."[3]

Tears

Somé believes that the salty taste of tears, the recognition and release of our grief, is good. He calls it "the cleansing taste of reconciliation" between what is possible and not—"of the desire to reconcile, because water cleanses and washes away the impurities of our failures. Grief is the enemy of denial. An elder once said: 'My tears say that my soul has heard something about the Other World.'"

The Gambia's Sacred Pool

In the West African country of The Gambia is a sacred pool that has become a major attraction for foreign visitors. Situated in the tourist town of Bakau, eight miles from the capital city of Banjul, the pool was discovered hundreds of years ago by the native people. The pool is home to more than 100 crocodiles—and to a fertility rite that is gaining steadily in international renown.

Hundreds of infertile women travel from far and wide, from both within and outside The Gambia, to visit this site, where they are washed with sacred water in the pool by specially trained women in the Bojang clan—the keepers of the pool. The resident crocodiles prefer fish to human flesh, and a very tame crocodile named Charlie often leaves the pool to spend time in the ancestral home of the Bojang clan. According to the pool attendant, when Charlie emerges it is usually a sign that he has a message for the people.

When rituals are performed in the pool, those washed in the sacred water are sternly warned to stick to their partners and avoid adultery. They are given a bottle of water from the pool that is to be applied to parts of the body before going to bed and early in the morning.

In return, people washed at the pool give offerings of cloth and coconuts. The elderly share half of the offering; the rest is thrown into the pool to appease the crocodiles. Once the ritual is performed, it is forbidden to shake hands with anybody from Bakau. Members of the Bojang clan are forbidden to exploit the pool for financial gain, lest it loses its sacredness. Quite a few of the tourists who have gone through the fertility ritual—many of whom are from the United Kingdom and Sweden—claim that it works.

Divine Water for Freedom

In Uganda in the first half of the twentieth century, water cults arose that involved drinking divine water, some of which had political overtones—namely, the overthrow of the Europeans. A famous prophet of the northern Kakwe people, Rembe, dispensed water that was imbued with mysterious power to his adherents. Rembe promised that the water would restore their damaged society by bringing dead livestock back to life, driving away disease and foreign newcomers, and making the drinkers immune to bullets.

A similar cult was found in southeastern and central Tanganyika during the famed Maji Maji rebellion (*maji* is Swahili for water) against the German colonial government. It was believed that those who drank the water would be immune to bullets and drive the Germans to the sea. This rebellion lasted from 1905 to 1907 and was stamped out only after 250,000 Africans had died and the prophet Kinjikitile, who had instigated the rebellion, was hung.[4]

Prosperity Ritual

The powers found in water can bring prosperity. A group of people seeking prosperity can build a small spirit boat. They decorate the boat as a group, with each person offering something of personal value in gratitude, together creating a boat of great beauty and shared meaning. After invocations that clearly specify what they are asking for—rather than a general request for prosperity—the boat is set into a river of running water that runs to the sea. The spirit of water absorbs the thought, the prayer, and the intention of the people; while carrying it to the sea, it spreads the wish out into the world for realization on the physical plane.

Water Bowl for Seeing

Somé's grandfather was the guardian of his village. At nighttime, while others slept, his grandfather could always determine whether the fields were being raided by wild animals. The device he used to keep vigil consisted of a clay pot filled with "virgin water," rainfall that had never touched the earth in its fall from the sky. Sitting alone in his clay-walled hut, he saw everything that happened throughout the farm by looking into this water.[5]

The Spirits that Live in African Waters

Nommo and the Rain Ceremony

The natives of Mali in West Africa say that water is inhabited by Nommo, a spirit endowed with mysterious, extraordinary, and sometimes frightening powers, to whom human beings owe total veneration. Nommo may bring the rain and guarantee men's prosperity, but he may also cause drought and misery, if men and women neglect to worship him. To this day in Burkina Faso, men and women celebrate the return of the rains by wearing large, colorful, butterfly-like masks, because butterflies always swarm out just after the rains.[6]

Obatala and the Creation of the World— Yoruba Tale of the Drunken Goddess

In the Yoruba religion of West Africa, one of the greatest *orishas* (deities) is Obatala, the creator deity who is both mother and father of wisdom. When this old legend is recited by Yoruba women, Obatala is a woman. One day she looks down from the heavens and discovers a ball of water suspended in space. Obatala decides to explore the water ball and, after going to her fellow orishas for advice and assistance, she creates the planet Earth using sand, seeds, a chicken, and a cat. After overindulging in palm wine, the lonely Obatala begins to build statues in memory of her fellow orishas. In darkness, drunkenness, and carelessness, Obatala creates statues of clay with tremendous differences—some with sight, some sightless; some black, some white; some walking, some lame; and so on. Without realizing this, she prays to Oladumare, the great orisha, supreme creator of the universe, to endow her statues with life. And thus, the human race is created.

African Spiritual Bathing in the Americas:
Take Me to the River

Baptism is one of the most enduring traditions of African-American Christian churches. The ritual action of immersion has long carried the hope of renewal and freedom, ideas that have always driven African-American spirituality.

Baptism has deep connections to African religions. Most American slaves were taken from West Africa, where river cults require ceremonies involving total immersion of the body. Even after being Christianized, slaves held onto some of their African traditions, incorporating elements of the new faith. The belief in ritual immersion as a vehicle for spiritual purification and renewal of purpose was one that Africans shared with Christians. (It's worth noting that in Nova Scotia, black baptism rituals evolved almost completely independently of influence from outside Christian religious authority.[7])

For many African-Americans, baptism is a symbolic ritual of purification and initiation and a washing away of evil, as well as a significant rite of passage for births, deaths, and marriages. The Beouf and Ouachita rivers near Monroe, Louisiana have been used for baptism for several generations.

During the summer, pastors gather their congregations for group river baptisms; congregants sing old traditional spirituals such as "Take Me to the River," "I Know I've Got Religion," and "Wade in the Water." These group baptisms are usually held after religious revivals in order to integrate newcomers into the church. Initiates are often dressed in white robes along with white headgear resembling a chef's hat or a simple white headband.

Usually one or more of the church deacons wades into the waist-high river water and invites the baptismal candidates to come forth one by one. While the other church members stand on the shore singing and encouraging the initiates, the minister gives the meaning of baptism by reciting from the third chapter of Matthew, which tells the story of John the Baptist and the biblical heritage of river baptism in the Jordan River. Then the minister folds each newcomer's hands in prayer, covers the face, and dips him or her into the river, saying, "I baptize this little sister [or brother], [name], in the name of the Father, in the name of the Son, and in the name of the Holy Ghost."

The congregation responds with joyous songs, tears, applause, and praise of the new converts. The church mothers meet them as they emerge from the river and blanket them with sheets and towels. The ceremony closes with a prayer circle at the water's edge, after which all retire to the church hall for a grand celebration feast.

Baba Ishangi's Summer Solstice Ritual

According to Baba Ishangi, an African folklorist, musician, and dancer, Africans commonly use the innate healing power of water, herbs, and prayer to create an atmosphere of spiritual cleanliness and to elevate minds to receive what is called in Nigerian *ashe,* the blessings of the Almighty. Ishangi believes that spiritual bathing opens people to prayer and meditation and heightens their ability to concentrate. It helps individuals, families, or whole communities to attain good luck, health, and prosperity, to erase negative vibrations, and to become a vehicle for divine intervention.

The African Diaspora Religions

The African diaspora religions, which share similar deities, migrated to this hemisphere along with enslaved Africans. These religions include Santeria, Macumba, Umbanda, Voudun (Voodoo), and Palo Mayombe. During slavery, the true African nature of these religions was disguised: the deities were clothed as Catholic saints and the worship was hidden in Catholic forms. Now, the worshippers can be more open about their true beliefs, and the deities have resumed their traditional African manifestations. These religions have millions of believers throughout Latin America, and many in the United States as well, especially in Florida and Louisiana.

Voudun has its roots in Yoruba ceremonies and religion; it was brought to Haiti by African slaves from Nigeria who later converted to Catholicism. One *lwa* or spirit (also known as Ogun, among other names) shares some of the qualities of St. John the Baptist.

Water is integral to Voudun ceremonies and prayers, since it serves as both a buffer zone between the world of spirit and the world of matter and a conduit of spiritual energy for travel between the two worlds.

Voudun is becoming popular with people of all ethnic backgrounds, not just people of African descent. In almost every American city one can find botanicas—stores selling supplies such as special candles for each deity, agua florida (a universally popular ingredient for ritual baths and floor washes), statues of the orishas, magical floorwashes, cascarilla (a medicinal plant), and all the supplies necessary to worship the orishas properly. Some botanicas also have priests or priestesses on duty, as well as elaborate shrines to the orishas where devotees may pray and leave offerings.

Rituals and ceremonies are conducted with the protection of the *priere Guinea,* the prayer of Africa, which begins: "Announce the angel in the water. O Creole, fathom the mirror, O Legba-e." This invites the participant to focus on spiritual energy that can enter into and act upon the material world, and to project his or her consciousness beyond the surface of the mirror and thus journey into the spiritual realm.

Ceremonies are opened by and center on the libations of water poured out before the four directions, the drums, and important ceremonial objects or areas. In some ceremonies, spirits or *lwas* are led in on streams of water, trickled from the entrance to the location of the drums.

Yemaya/Yemanja, Goddess of the Ocean

Yemaya or Yemanja is the goddess of the ocean, Mother of Fishes. She is a loving, maternal goddess who often saves her devotees from drowning; practitioners believe that it was Yemaya who saved the life of Elian Gonzales—the young Cuban boy who arrived in Florida in 1999 as the only survivor in a boatload of Cuban refugees—in answer to his mother's dying prayer.

Yemaya's colors are clear (or white) and blue. Yemaya's festival takes place each year on February 2 in Bahia, Brazil, where many thousands of people, dressed in the goddess's colors, go to the beach at dawn, bringing offerings of flowers, perfume, soap, candles, and jewelry. The festival reaches its climax when these offerings are carried out to sea on Yemaya's waves.

Other Voudun Water Goddesses

Oshun or Ochun is the goddess of the River Niger and the goddess of love and beauty. Flirtatious, beautiful, and sexy, Oshun is often depicted admiring herself in a mirror—and is often invoked for help in love matters.

Erzulie or Ezili is the Voudun goddess of water, streams, and waterfalls. Erzulie has many aspects. Erzulie Dantor appears as a dark mother with tribal scars on her face; Erzulie Freda appears as a white woman and is identified with the Virgin Mary.

La Sirene is the Mermaid Goddess of Voudun, the Great Mother.

Mama Chola or Choya Wengue is the Spirit of River, an Enkisi (deity) invoked for love magic, all things sexy and erotic.

Madre Agua or Kalunga is the Mother of the Ocean, a gentle and loving Enkisi who is the patroness of mothers and children; she is also a great healer.

VODOO SPIRITUAL BATHING RITUALS

Magic Foot Track Wash

There is an African belief in "foot-track magic," which causes good or evil to enter into another through their feet as they walk over buried or hidden objects that have been ritually imbued with harmful intent. Regular ritual bathing is needed to remove the harmful effects.

Ritual Floor-Washing

Ritual floor-washing is yet another custom that can rid a house of evil influences, prevent evil from entering the house, and bring in good luck, success, or happiness. To attract good fortune, the floor is washed with an inward motion, from the walls to the center; to eliminate evil, it is washed with an outward motion, from the center to the walls. The wash water usually contains saltpeter, herbal or floral essences, and table salt; agua florida is also used. The wash water should be thrown away into the front yard toward the east, preferably into the sunrise.

The Kanzo Ceremony

Many modern-day believers and practitioners of Voudun believe that a ritual bath will put an end to adverse conditions and open the way for luck, love, money, and happiness to enter their lives.

Initiates taking part in a ceremony known as *kanzo* are given no fewer than twenty-one herb and water baths. Once finished with the kanzo ceremony, initiates are forbidden to submerge their entire head in a river or the sea, because this gives water *lwas* such as Simbi or La Sirene the best possible opportunity to induce possession and steal the initiate away for seven years' service.

St. John's Eve Baptism

Most Voudun temples adhere to the practice of a baptism-like ceremony on June 23, the revered day known as St. John's Eve (Midsummer's Eve). The faithful are anointed or sprinkled with hyssop-infused water or rum by a *mambo* or Voudun priestess.[8]

Hyssop Bath

Perhaps the best-known herb for spiritual bathing in the African-American Christian and Voudun community is hyssop. Mentioned in Psalm 51 of the Bible as the herb to use for purification from negative influences, hyssop was used by the ancient Jews.

Practitioners boil or soak hyssop in water, then bathe a person suffering from a spiritual illness. They may also sprinkle the herbal water around the entire compound of the house or apartment to rid the area of evil influences. Bathers are asked to repeat the baths seven times over seven days while saying seven prayers. The same ritual might be repeated three or nine times, depending on the belief and number preference of the Voudun practitioner.

MORE SPIRITUAL BATHING RITUALS

Water Bowl Ritual

Leave a bowl of water someplace where you spend time—such as your home or office. Place a bowl of water in a room where a difficult discussion or meeting is to take place. This can have a remarkable effect on the tone of the interaction. The very presence of water near us is calming and promotes peace and reconciliation.

Libation Ritual

Libation means pouring out a small quantity of water as an offering to anyone in the Spirit World for the purposes of encouraging peace and togetherness.[9] It is a maintenance ritual that can be done at any time.

Some Africans believe that any water poured to the ancestors or spirit beings is received in the Other World for the purpose of providing peaceful continuity. Establish a sacred altar in your house and go there every morning with a fresh glass of water. Sitting or kneeling at the altar, hold the water in your hand and pray to the spirit of the ancestors and to any spirit being you know, inviting them to be the main artisans of the day ahead of you. It is useful to give as much detail as possible about what the content of the day is going to be, including any meetings or events that are very important to you; you can even express things such as your concerns about commuting in traffic. You can also pour a little water on the altar and ask the ancestors to use it as a peaceful umbrella to protect against the heat of misfortune, bad luck, and disappointment. Leave a glass or bowl of water on the altar at all times to indicate your desire for peace, reconciliation, and focus in that place.

Summer Solstice Community Baptism

The all-night ritual begins at 11 p.m. on a Friday closest to the summer solstice.
Gather at a local church and bring a gospel choir and sacred drums.
Pray, meditate, and give thanksgiving until 5 a.m.
Make your way to a local beach via car caravan.
Immerse completely in the water, accompanied by further prayer, drumming, dancing, and general celebration.
If there is a spiritual leader, kneel with him or her in the waters of *Yemanja/Olokun*—Yoruba names for the ocean and her depths.

Flower Baths

Instructions for Making Flower Baths

Many of the spiritual baths in this book call for gathering flowers or plants while repeating certain prayers or maintaining a certain state of mind. So, follow these general instructions for each recipe that includes the gathering of plants or the saying of prayers.

There are truly countless plants and flowers that can be called into service to create a spiritually healing bath. The list on page 168 includes popular and recommended plants; you'll find some of them at the grocery store or even in your kitchen spice cabinet. While this list is by no means complete, it is a good start and gives you a sense of how many different plants lend themselves to spiritual bathing. Planning a spiritual bath is a great opportunity to educate yourself about the wild plants in your area or yard with medicinal properties you haven't known about.

Be sure to select only flowers that have not been sprayed with insecticides. And as you collect from living plants, be mindful of their needs for survival and seed production to ensure the next generation. Do not stress plants by taking more than they can give.

Gather sprigs, flowers, and leaves with special care and consideration, much as you would borrow from a special friend of whom you are asking a favor. They should be collected with the Herb Collector's Prayer of Faith and Thanksgiving, which was given to us by the late Don Elijio Panti, the great Maya shaman of Belize:

> "In the name of the Father, the Son, and the Holy Ghost, I give thanks to the spirit of this plant, and I have faith with all my heart that it will help to make a wonderfully healing bath for me" [or name of the person you are preparing the bath for].

Place the fresh plant parts—whether leaves or flowers—in a basin in the sun for three hours. Crush the plants with your hands in the water until the water takes on a greenish color and the plant parts are well mashed. In the wintertime you can use dried plants; this is a good reason to dry wild or cultivated plants, such as marigolds, roses, hollyhocks, lavender, hyssop, oregano, and basil. If you use dried plants, prepare at least one cup for a bath.

Pour two quarts of boiling water over the plants, cover, and allow them to steep for thirty minutes. Once the water is at a comfortable temperature, pour it into the bathtub or pour it over your body from a dipper.

Once the bath is under way, pray and focus on your intention and on what you are trying to accomplish. What change would you like to see happen in your life? What would you like to eliminate from your life? What particular physical or emotional healing do you need? If you're preparing the bath for another person, consider what your friend or client needs at this time. The clearer you are about this, the better the results will be. If you're not really in need of anything special, but would like to take a spiritual bath just for the experience, that's fine, too.

Many of these bath rituals call for prayer or meditation. Choose a favorite prayer of your faith.

Reccomended Leaves and Flowers

Artemisia	Meadowsweet	Mullein
Lemon balm	Hollyhock	Chamomile
Basil	Yellow dock	Oregano
Thyme	Horsetail	Bay leaves
Chickweed	Elderflowers	Pine needles
Linden	Hyssop	Plantain
Citrus	Blessed thistle	Poppies
Catnip	Marigold	Red or white rose
Cleavers	Lavender	Vervain
Yarrow	Motherwort	St. John's wort
Comfrey	Chicory	Burdock

Florecidas at Home

Gather nontoxic flowers from your garden, a field of wildflowers, or (with permission!) a neighbor's yard. While you're picking the flower heads, be sure to visualize and send love and appreciation to them.

Collect about two handfuls of fresh flower heads or flowering stems. Some suggestions are red or white roses, marigolds, zinnias, hollyhocks, linden flowers, cosmos, lilacs, hibiscus, lavender, sage, or thyme. If only one type is available, that's fine.

Place the flowers in a pot or a basin of water containing one to two gallons of water. While praying or stating your intention for the healing bath, squeeze the flowers between your hands until they are well mashed and the water takes on their color and aroma.

If time allows, place the flowers and water in the sun for one to three hours. If possible, it is nice to do this bath outdoors, sitting in the sunlight and allowing your body to air-dry afterward. If not, take the container of water and flowers into the shower; you can strain out the coarse material first if necessary. It is nice to gather up the flower parts and rub them onto your face and body, if you can do so without putting strain on your body. With a nonbreakable dipper, pour the water over your entire body while praying or meditating on the desired result. It's best not to dry with a towel; let the florecida air-dry while you sit and pray. Be sure to keep warm.

Water can also absorb the energy vibrations from music, so why not play some soothing classical pieces, chants, or chakra-balancing sounds while soaking in your sacred bath water?

Group Flower Baths

This is an extremely popular group healing activity, much loved by those who attend the healing seminars at Ix Chel Farm in Belize. All you need is a set of clean buckets and enough plants and flowers for all.

Give each person a bucket and instruct them in the importance of saying prayers of thanksgiving and faith to the plants and the flowers as they are collected.

Each person collects a predetermined number of plants. The number should be one that resonates with them for personal reasons. Most choose four, seven, or nine, but any number will do, and a bath with one single plant is also fine.

Collect three, four, or nine flowers or leaves from each plant, depending on how much the plant has to give to the group as a whole. Each person should end up with about half a bucketful of fresh plants and flowers. Remove any larger branches. Fill each bucket halfway with water, then send each person to a place where he or she can sit comfortably to squeeze and mash the leaves and flowers by hand while praying and infusing the water with need and intention. When participants are finished, the plant parts should be well mashed and the water should have taken on a deep, rich green color.

This can be either scooped out immediately and—in a secluded area away from observers or passersby—poured over the entire body, or allowed to sit in the sun for one to three hours before being slathered on.

It's really nice to do this outside on a warm, sunny day. Splashing and throwing water at each other is fun and energetically cleanses a wider area. However, most people want to be alone to meditate and enjoy that special feeling of inner contentment that comes after the bath. It is best to allow the body to air-dry, but be sure to avoid drafts and cold breezes.

Baths for Cranky, Upset Babies

These work wonders on the little darlings, especially when they won't sleep or seem out of sorts for no discernible reason. The Maya believe the baths soothe and calm babies who are missing a family member or who have experienced a fright caused by a loud noise or a fall, or witnessing a traumatic event.

Your best choices for baby baths are leaves or flowers of marigold (not the calendula), basil, St. John's wort, rosemary, or red or white roses. Collect about a quart of fresh plants of your choice on a sunny day. Be sure to choose plants free of toxic sprays or chemicals. Fill a bucket with two gallons of water and squeeze the chosen plants into the water for five to ten minutes, until they are well mashed and the water takes on a vibrant color.

Set this in the sun until it warms nicely. If baby is big enough to sit up, pour the floral water into her baby bath and let her play in this water for twenty to thirty minutes. Otherwise, hold the baby in one arm while pouring the water over her body with an unbreakable dipper. Take her out and dry her with a warmed towel.

In the winter, bring two gallons of water to a boil and steep a cup of any of the plants mentioned above for twenty minutes. When the water is comfortably and safely warm, strain it and pour into baby's bath, then proceed as above.

Voilà! You won't believe the difference. Repeat as often as desired.

Hand and Foot Baths

Both our hands and feet absorb energy easily, so it might as well be energy of a healing nature whenever possible. These baths work wonders; they are easy to prepare and offer another good way to work with a group.

Follow the general instructions for preparing a basin or a bucket of flower water—but note, for this bath dried plants will not replace the vital energy of living flowers. When your water, plants, and prayers are ready, arrange a comfortable seat at a table. Where your feet will rest, place a towel on top of a bath rug. Put most of the warmed bath water in a container with room for your feet, deep enough for the water to reach up to your calves. Pour the rest of the water into a basin in which to soak your hands; place this on the table. Put on some smooth and easy music. Now, soak your feet and hands while sitting quietly and allowing the experience to soak in. Many relate that they can feel strong, pleasant waves pulsing through their hands and feet. A good time to meditate and pray.

A Bath to Relieve Anxiety

This is also very good for those who have had insomnia or troubling dreams. Use leaves and or flowers of hyssop, lavender, chamomile, lemon-balm, and St. John's wort, either fresh or dried. You can choose only one or as many as you can find. Prepare according to the general instructions. You will need a gallon of prepared water to pour into a bathtub filled with nicely warmed water.

You can strain or not strain, depending on the plumbing. If you don't have to strain, it is really wonderful to soak amidst the swirling plants; gather them up in your hands and enjoy the aroma. It's also nice to rub a handful into your skin and squeeze out their juices. Soak in the warm tub for twenty to thirty minutes, dipping into the bath water with a container and pouring it over your head every few minutes. An alternate method is to pour the warmed water over yourself in the shower. Try to clear your mind of worry or anxiety; when it does steal back in, continually repeat a prayer, such as "Thy will be done."

Aromatic candles are a nice touch.

A Prayerful Bath

Fill your tub with water as usual. Put on some soft, classical music or chanting tapes. Light a few candles, burn some incense, and climb in. Place a cushion or towel behind your head so that you can comfortably recline with your mouth just above the water line. Chant or pray according to your personal belief system. Allow the words to float into the water—you will actually see the waves of sound flowing all around you, bathing you in the power of the divine word. Hmmmmm.

Color Healing Baths

Colors vibrate at different frequencies that relate to the different emotional and spiritual needs of human beings. Water absorbs these light frequencies, stores them, and transmits them into, over, and through our energy fields as we bathe.

For a color healing bath you'll need bottles or glasses of various colors. Red glass increases energy, leadership, and vitality. Lavender helps with anxiety and stress, thereby boosting the immune system. Blue glass is calming and relaxing, good for those who need to slow down or adjust after a time of overly vigorous activity. Yellow glass stimulates the mind and helps you shake off mental dullness. Green can be healing and energizing—wine bottles work well. You can use a drinking glass, a quart jar, or a bottle as large as a gallon.

Pour regular tap water or spring water into the colored container of your choice. While filling the container, contemplate your intention for this ritual. A prayer will do nicely, too. Add gemstones such as crystals for more energy enhancement.

Place in the sun for three to eight hours. Drink eight ounces and, if you used a large container, pour the remaining charged water over your body. Alternatively, you can drink some and store the rest in the refrigerator to take in eight-ounce doses daily. This can also be a multipurpose lustral water (water that you have prayed over) that you can drink as you need, offer to a friend, sprinkle around the house, or add to your bath.

Salt and Water Cleansing Ritual for Bodyworkers

This is a simple way to cleanse your body and hands of emotionally charged energy, either after doing bodywork on clients who experienced an emotional release during the session, or when you sense that you have absorbed some negative energy from the person. If you're in a hurry, simply dip your hands into a basin of sea salt and water as if washing your hands. Instead of drying your hands, sprinkle some of the salt water on your head and over your body.

When you've had a really difficult day with clients, pour a half cup of sea salt into the bathtub, fill it with nice, warm water, and soak for ten minutes, rinsing off with fresh, plain water afterward. Be sure to have a dipper at hand to pour water over your head several times during the bath.

Gemstone Baths

Take a cue from the ancient Egyptians, who ground gemstones in water and then drank this as an elixir. If you use crystals, this is a good way to enhance your relationship with them and introduce more of their healing and balancing energy into your life. Crystals, like water, give back to us what we put into them. So to enhance your energy after strenuous physical or emotional times, sit with your crystal and meditate on well-being and emotional poise. Soak your crystal in a glass bowl or drinking glass (no need to grind it up!) in the sun for just an hour. Remove the crystal and pour this over your body all at once, or store in the refrigerator for up to two weeks. You can drink a few ounces at a time as an energizing and spiritually harmonizing elixir or add some to bath water, a little at a time.

Cleansing Baths for Your Gemstones

Because crystals and gemstones absorb and transmit our energies and intentions back to us, they too, need occasional spiritual bathing. You can soak them in lustral water in a clear bowl or glass in the light of the full moon or full sun. Add a teaspoon of sea salt for further clearing.

Mayan healers cleanse their crystals—called *sastuns*—on Thursdays and Fridays with changes of the moon cycle. They dip the index finger of the right hand into some rum or sea water and make nine crosses over the crystal while saying nine prayers, usually the Lord's Prayer.

Afterword

There is far more to spiritual bathing than the few scattered religious or folk rituals of which most of us are aware! This deeply healing, connecting, and soul-fulfilling practice is a powerful prism through which to learn about and understand the world's cultures and religions. It is one of those mysterious spiritual threads that connects all of humanity—east, west, north, and south, from ancient through contemporary times.

Each tradition has its own philosophy, prayers, mythology, and rituals, and something unique to teach us about how humanity has lived and survived on our planet. Yet within this diversity we found commonality: We are amazed by the similar practices and concepts shared by the peoples who populate different parts of the earth.

Throughout our journey, we have been constantly reminded of the wisdom of the late comparative religion scholar Mircea Eliade: It was he who reminded us that through studying the traditions of other peoples, we deepen our understanding of our own.

Endnotes

Components of Spiritual Bathing

1 Alec Croutier, *Taking the Waters: Spirit, Art, Sensuality,* Abbeville Publishing Group, New York. 2000.

2 Ibid.

3 Charlie Ryrie, "The Healing Energy of Waters," *Journey Editions,* Boston, 1999.

4 Jeane Manning, "The Power of Water, Atlantis Rising," #19, 1999.

5 Margarita Artschwager Kay, *Healing with Plants in the American and Mexican West.*

The Jews

1 Geraldine Sherman, "Total Immersion," *Toronto Life,* November 1997.

2 Rivkah Slonim, "Understanding the Mikvah and Laws of Family Purity," *Congregation Agdas Achim Chabad,* Jason Aronson Inc., Northvale, NJ.

3 Rabbi Geraldine Sherman, "Total Immersion," *Toronto Life,* November 1997.

4 Mikvah Preparation List, Adas Isreal, Washington D.C.

5 Part of the Adas Israel Congregation Collection, Washington D.C.

6 Rabbi Lawrence Kushner, *The River of Light.*

7 First published in Cracow in 1577. Translation by Chava Weissler from the Basle 1602 edition.

The Sumerians, Mandaeans, and Egyptians

1 *Encyclopedia of World Religions,* Ablutions.

2 www.farvardyn.com/mandaean1.htm, abstracted from the Mandaeans of Iraq and Iran by E. S. Drower, Leiden 1962.

3 *Encyclopedia of World Religions,* Water.

4 *Encyclopedia Britannica,* Nun and Naunet, "Deities of Chaos and Water" by Caroline Seawright, Tour Egypt.

5 *Encyclopedia of World Religions,* Water.

6 Ibid.

7 *Encylopedia of World Religion,* Rivers.

8 Based on an interview with Caroline Kenner, Washington D.C.

9 *Encyclopedia of World Religions,* Ablutions, Volume 1.

10 Ibid.

The Christian World

1 Mark 1:7-11.

2 Luke 1:4-6.

3 John 3:5.

4 Rom 6:4.

5 Mary Rourke, "These Waters Run Deep," *The Los Angeles Times.*

6 *The Incarnate God: The Feast of Jesus Christ and the Virgin Mary, Volume 1,* Catherine Aslanoff, ed., St. Vladimir Seminary Press, 1995.

7 *Encyclopedia Britannica,* Holy Water.

8 Ibid.

Ancient Romans and Greeks

1 Yegul, Fikret, *Baths & Bathing in Classical Antiquity,* MIT Press, Cambridge, MA, 1992.

2 S. Giedion, "Architecture and the Phenomena of Transition," quoted in Yegel, Frikert, *Baths & Bathing in Classical Antiquity,* MIT Press, Cambridge, MA, 1992.

3 Yegul, Fikret, *Baths & Bathing in Classical Antiquity,* MIT Press, Cambridge, MA, 1992.

4 Barbara Walker, *The Woman's Encyclopedia of Myths and Secrets,* Harper & Row, San Francisco, 1983.

5 Alev Croutier, *Taking the Waters: Spirit, Art, Sensuality,* Abbeville Publishing Group, New York., 2000.

6 Barbara Walker, *The Woman's Encyclopedia of Myths and Secrets,* Harper & Row, San Francisco, 1983.

7 Mikkel Aaland, "Mediterranean Baths; The Early Greek and Roman Baths," www.cyberbohemia.com/Pages/EarlyGreek.htm.

8 Yegul, Friket, *Baths & Bathing in Classical Antiquity*. MIT Press, Cambridge, MA, 1992.

9 Alev Croutier, *Taking the Waters: Spirit, Art, Sensuality*, Abbeville Publishing Group, New York, 2000.

10 Ibid.

11 Salomon Reinach, *Orpheus: A History of Religions*, Liveright Publishing Company, New York, 1942. "Rites of Aspersion."

The Muslims

1 Attributed to Muhammad, quoted by Mircea Eliade from M. M. Ali, *A Manual of Hadith*, Lahore, 1994.

2 Mircea Eliade, *Encylopedia of World Religions*, Ablutions, Vol. 1, p. 10.

3 *The Concise Encyclopedia of Islam*.

4 Mikkel Aaland, "Mediterranean Baths: The Islamic Hammam Is Born," www.cyberbohemia.com/Pages/Islahammam.htm.

The Celts, Druids, and Wiccans

1 Colin Renfrew, *Archaeology and Language: The Puzzle of Indo-European Origins*.

2 Miranda Green, *Celtic Myths*, British Museum Press, 1993.

3 Ibid.

4 R. Hutton, *The Triumph of the Moon*, Oxford, England, Oxford University Press, 1999.

5 Miranda Green, *Celtic Myths*, British Museum Press, 1993.

6 John Michell, *The Traveler's Key to Sacred England: A Guide to the Legend, Lore and Landscape of England's Sacred Places*, Gothic Image, 2003.

7 www.MythingLink.com.

8 Ibid.

9 Rowan, *Buttons, Bras, and Pins: The Folklore of British Holy Wells*.

10 Miranda Green, *Celtic Myths*, British Museum Press, 1993.

11 C. Ryrie, *The Healing Energies of Water*, Journey Editions, Boston, 1999, p. 38.

12 Ibid.

13 Barbara Walker, *The Woman's Encyclopedia of Myths and Secrets,*.

14 Ibid.

15 Ibid.

16 A Druid named Norfolk, founder of Cornish Earth Mysteries, meynmamvro@freeserve.co.uk.

17 Sarolta G. DeFaltay Deep Skies Astrological Services http://moonspells.com 1997-2003.

The Finns and Russians

1 Leena Maunula, "A Journey into Steam Baths on Three Continents," Helsingin Sanomat, http://www.helsinki-hs.net/thisweek/03112000.html.

2 Mikkel Aaland, "History of the Nordic Bath, Sweat," www.cyberbohemia.com/Pages/historyofnordic.htm.

3 Mikkel Aaland, "The Russian Bania: History of the Great Russian Bath," from *Sweat: An Illustrated History of the Sauna and Sweatbath in Finland and Other Cultures*, 1978.

4 Ibid.

5 Ibid.

6 *The Boston Globe*, April 24, 2002.

7 Mikkel Aaland, "The Russian Bania: History of the Great Russian Bath," from *Sweat: An Illustrated History of the Sauna and Sweatbath in Finland and Other Cultures*, 1978.

The Native Americans

1 Leena Maunula, "A Journey into Steam Baths on Three Continents," Helsingin Sanomat, http://www.helsinki-hs.net/thisweek/03112000.html.

2 Mikkel Aaland, 1997. "Joining Running Foot in a Navajo Sweat Lodge," http://www.cyberbohemia.com/Pages/joiningrf.htm.

3 Argus Leader, "Building Your Own Sweat Lodge."

4 Mikkel Aaland, "Native American Sweat Lodge. The Sweat Lodge Joins the Modern World." www.cyberbohemia.com/Pages/joinsmodern.htm.

The Maya

1 Freidel, David, Linda Schele, Joy Parker. *Maya Cosmos: Three Thousand Years on the Shaman's Path*, New York, Morrow, 1993.

2 Joseph Campbell states in his book, *The Power of Myth*, that the number nine is where the spiritual manifests

on the physical plane. There are four bacabs that hold up the four corners of the universe, there are four directions, and some of their gods have four aspects. For instance, Ix Chel is the goddess of healing, weaving, the moon, and childbirth.

3 David Freidel, Linda Schele, Joy Parker. *Maya Cosmos: Three Thousand Years on the Shaman's Path*, Morrow, New York, 1993.

4 Ibid.

5 Ibid.

The Aztecs

1 In the temezcal, wrote the fifteenth-century Catholic priest Fray Bernardino de Sahagun, the sick "restore their bodies, their nerves. Those who are faint with sickness are there calmed, strengthened."

The Hindus

1 Vidya Dehjejia, et al., *Devi: The Great Goddess*, Arthur M. Sackler Gallery, 1999, Washington, D.C..

2 This contradiction of a life-giving and destroying deity was established in the frightening image of Kali, the destroyer, who absorbs all dead things into herself to allow for the renewal and regeneration of life.

Buddhism

1 Peter Grilli, *Furo: The Japanese Bath*, Kodansha International Limited, 1985.

2 Ibid.

3 National Museum of Japanese History http://www.rekihaku.ac.jp

4 Ibid.

5 Peter Grilli, *Furo: The Japanese Bath*, Kodansha International Limited, 1985.

6 Ibid.

7 Ibid.

8 *Asian Art and Culture*, Arthur M. Sackler Gallery, Smithsonian Institution, 1995.

9 Charlie Ryrie, *The Healing Energies of Water*, Journey Editions, Boston/Tokyo 1999.

10 "Bathhouse of the Floating World," *Furo: The Japanese Bath*, Kodansha International Limited, 1985.

The Thais, Cambodians, and Chinese

1 Rachada Rithdee, "The Rhythm of Water," *Sawasdee*, April.

2 Pijew Dejpiw, "Wet Lunar Blessings," *The Nation*, Bangkok, April 13, 2002.

3 *Asian Art and Culture*, Arthur M. Sackler Gallery, Smithsonian Institution, 1995.

4 Jean Chevalier and Alain Buchanan-Brown, *The Penguin Dictionary of Symbols*, Penguin 1996.

The Africans

1 Malidoma Patrice Somé, *The Healing Wisdom of Africa: Finding Life Purpose Through Nature, Ritual and Community*, Tarcher/Putnam, New York, 1999.

2 Ibid.

3 Ibid.

4 *EWR*, East African Religions: An Overview.

5 Malidoma Patrice Somé, *Of Water and the Spirit*, Penguin, New York, 1995.

6 Djenaba Kouyate, "Women in West African Folklore" *Texas Teller*, February 1995, www.tejasstorytelling.com.

7 Camilla L. Greene, *Myth Connections*, Yale-New Haven Teachers Institute.

8 *Times-Picayune*, New Orleans, June 30, l999.

9 Malidoma Patrice Somé, *The Healing Wisdom of Africa: Finding Life Purpose Through Nature, Ritual and Community*, Tarcher/Putnam, New York. 1999.

Bibliography

Aaland, Mikkel. 1978. Sweat. www.cyberbohemia.com

Allegro, John Marco. *People of the Dead Sea Scrolls*. New York: Doubleday & Co., Inc., 1958.

Altman, Nathaniel. *Sacred Water: The Spiritual Source of Life*. Mahwah, NJ: Hidden Spring Press, 2002.

Arvigo, Rosita, and Nadine Epstein. *Rainforest Remedies: The Maya Way to Heal Your Soul and Nourish Your Body*. San Francisco: Harper San Francisco, 2001.

Asian Art and Culture, Arthur M. Sackler Gallery, Smithsonian Institute, Spring/Summer 1995.

Aslanoff, Catherine, ed. *The Incarnate God, The Feasts of Jesus Christ and the Virgin Mary*. Vol. 1. Crestwood, NY: St. Vladimir's Seminary Press, 1995.

Austin, Milli D. *The Healing Bath*. Rochester, VT: Healing Arts Press, 1997.

Badianus Manuscript. *An Aztec Herbal of 1552*. Baltimore: John Hopkins University Press, 1940.

Banks, Natalie. *The Golden Thread*. London: Lucis Press, 1963.

Baudez, Claude, and Sydney Picasso. *Lost Cities of the Maya*. New York: Harry N. Abrams, Inc., 1992.

Beckwith, Carol, and Angela Fisher. *African Ceremonies*. Vol. 1 and 2. New York: Harry N. Abrams, 1999.

Benedetti, Maria Dolores. *Hasta los Banos Te Curan!* Maplewood, NJ: Waterfront Press, 1991.

Brockman, Norbert. *Encyclopedia of Sacred Places*. New York: Oxford University Press, 1997.

Buttrick et al., ed. *The Interpreter's Bible*. Vol. 8. New York: Abingdon Press, 1952.

Cahill, Thomas. *How The Irish Saved Civilization*. Landover Hills, MD: Anchor Publishing, 1996.

Campbell, Joseph. *The Hero With a Thousand Faces*. Princeton: Princeton University, 1968.

Chevalier, Jean, and Alain Gheerbrant. *The Penguin Dictionary of Symbols*, 2nd ed. London: Penguin, 1969.

Childs, Craig. *The Secret Knowledge of Water*. Seattle: Sasquatch Books, 2000.

Connelly, Diane M. *Traditional Acupuncture: The Law of the Five Elements*. New York: New Directions Publishing, 1971.

Croutier, Alev Lytle. *Taking the Waters: Spirit, Art, Sensuality*. New York: Abbeville Press, 2000.

Davies, Nigel. *The Aztecs*. London: Abacus, 1977.

Day, A., and K. Davis. *Water: The Mirror of Science*. New York: Doubleday & Co., 1961.

Dehijia, Vidya, et al. *Devi: The Great Goddess*. Washington, DC: Arthur M. Sackler Gallery, Smithsonian Institution, 1999.

Denny, F. M. *An Introduction to Islam*. New York: Macmillan Publishing Co., 1994.

Diamant, Anita. *The New Jewish Wedding*. New York: Simon & Schuster, 2001.

Djpiw, Pichet. "Wet Lunar Blessings." *The Nation*, Focus Travel, 2002.

Dossey, Larry, M.D. *Healing Words: The Power of Prayer and the Practice of Medicine*. San Francisco: Harper San Francisco, 1993.

Eddy, Mary Baker. *Miscellaneous Writings, 1883-1896*. Boston, 1896.

Eiseley, Loren. *The Immense Journey*. New York: Time Reading Program, 1957.

Eliade, Mircea. *From Muhammed to Medicine Men*. New York: Harper & Row, 1967.

Eliade, Mercea, et al. *The Encyclopedia of Religion*, New York: Macmillan Publishing Co., 1987.

Eliade, Mircea, *Patterns in Comparative Religion*. New York: Sheed & Ward, 1999.

Frazer, Sir James George. *The New Golden Bough*. New Jersey: S. G. Phillips, Inc., 1965.

Friedel, David, Linda Schele, and Joy Parker. *Maya Cosmos: Three Thousand Years on the Shaman's Path*. New York: William Morrow, 1993.

Gadon, Elinor W. *The Once and Future Goddess*. New York: Harper & Row, 1989.

Graves, Robert. *Greek Myths*. Garden City, New York: Doubleday & Company, Inc., 1981.

Green, Miranda. *Celtic Myths*. London: British Museum Press, 1993.

Greene, Brian. *The Elegant Universe*. New York: W. W. Norton & Co., 1999.

Grilli, Peter. *Furo: The Japanese Bath*. Kodansha International Limited, 1985.

Harvey, Graham, ed. *Indigenous Religions, A Companion*. London and New York: Cassell Publishers, 2000.

Heilman, Samuel C. *When A Jew Dies*. Berkeley: University of California Press, 2001.

Hobson, Drake, and Davis, ed. *The Concise Encyclopedia of Islam*. San Francisco: Harper & Row, 1989.

Hopman, Ellen Evert. *A Druid's Herbal*. Rochester, VT: Destiny Books, 1995.

Hunter, Bruce C. *A Guide to Ancient Maya Ruins*. Norman, OK: University of Oklahoma Press., 1986.

Hutton, Ronald. *The Triumph of the Moon*. Oxford: Oxford University Press, 1999.

Jenkins, Elizabeth B. *Initiation*. New York: Berkeley Books, 1997.

Katz, Friedrich. *The Ancient American Civilizations*. London: Weidenfeld and Nicolson, 1972.

Keegan, Lynn, and Gerald Keegan. *Healing Waters*. New York: Berkeley Publishing Group, 1998

Kula, Rabbi, and Vanessa Ochs , Ph.D. *The Book of Jewish Sacred Practices*. Woodstock, VT: Jewish Light Publishing Co., 2001.

Littleton, C. Scott, ed. *Mythology: The Illustrated Anthology of World Myth and Storytelling*. London: Duncan Baird Publishers, 2002.

Marnham, Patrick. *Lourdes, A Modern Pilgrimage*. New York: Coward, McCann & Geoghegan, Inc., 1981.

Matt, Daniel C. *The Essential Kabbalah: The Heart of Jewish Mysticism*. San Francisco: Harper San Francisco, 1996.

Michell, John. *The Traveler's Key to Sacred England: A Guide to the Legends, Lore, and Landscape of England's Sacred Places*. New York: Knopf, 1999.

Mickaharic, Draja. *A Century of Spells*. York Beach, ME: Samuel Weiser, 1988.

Milojevic, Michael. "Forming and Transforming Proto-Byzantine Urban Public Space." www.mcauley.acu.edu.au/aabs/milo.htm

Molyneaux, Brian Leigh. *The Sacred Earth*. New York: Little Brown & Co., 1995.

O'Shea, William J. *The Sacraments of Initiation*. New Jersey: Prentice-Hall, 1965.

Ouspensky, L., and Vladimir Lossky. *The Meaning of Icons*. Crestwood, New York: St. Vladimir's Seminary Press, 1989.

Parrinder, Geoffrey. *African Mythology*. London: Hamlyn Publishing Group, Ltd., 1967.

Peredo, Miguel Guzman. *Medical Practices in Ancient America*. Mexico, copyright by Miguel Guzman Peredo, 1992.

Proskouriakoff, Tatiana. *An Album of Maya Architecture*. Norman, OK: University of Oklahoma Press, 1988.

Reinach, Salomon. *Orpheus: A History of Religions*. New York: Liveright Publishing Co., 1942.

Roberts, Karen. *The Flower Boy*. London: Phoenix House, 1999.

Ryrie, Charles. *The Healing Energies of Water*. Boston: Journey Traditions, 1999.

Scheffer, Mechthild. *The Encyclopedia of Bach Flower Therapy*. Rochester, VT: Healing Arts Press, 1999.

Schmemann, Alexander. *For the Life of the World*. New York: Athens Printing Company, 1973.

Schmemann, Alexander. *Of Water and the Spirit*. Crestwood, NY: St. Vladimir's Seminary Press, 1995.

Schimmel, Annemarie. *Mystical Dimensions of Islam*. Chapel Hill, NC: University of North Carolina Press, 1975.

The Shengold Jewish Encyclopedia. Rockville, MD: Schreiber Publishers, 2001.

Shepherd, A. P. *Rudolf Steiner: Scientist of the Invisible*. Rochester, VT: Inner Traditions. 1954.

Sherman, Rabbi Geraldine. "Total Immersion." *Toronto Life,* Nov. 1997.

Slonim, Rivkah. *Understanding the Mikvah and Laws of Family Purity*. Northvale, NJ: Congregation Agdas Achim Chabad, Jason Aronson, Inc.

Sloyan, Gerald S., ed. *Foundations of Catholic Theology Series*.

Smith, Huston. *The Illustrated World's Religions*. United Kingdom: Labyrinth Publishing Co. Ltd., 1994.

Smith, Huston. *World Religions*. San Francisco: Harper San Francisco, 1994.

Somé, Malidoma Patrice. *Of Water and the Spirit*. New York: Compass, 1995.

Steiner, Rudolf. *Theosophy*. New York: Anthroposophic Press, 1971.

Tompkins, Peter, and Christopher Bird. *The Secret Life of Plants*. New York: Avon Books, 1972.

Tooker, Elisabeth, ed. *Native North American Spirituality of the Eastern Woodlands*. New York: Paulist Press, 1979.

Vogel, V. J. *American Indian Medicine*. Norman, OK: University of Oklahoma Press, 1970.

Walker, Barbara. *The Woman's Encyclopedia of Myths and Secrets*. San Francisco: Harper & Row, 1983.

Weor, Samael Aun. *Tratado de Medicina Oculta y Magia Practica*. 1978.

Wood, Janie, and Tara Seefeldt. *The Wicca Cookbook: Recipes, Ritual and Lore*. Berkeley: Celestial Arts, 2000.

Wright, John W., ed. *The New York Times Almanac*. New York: Penguin Reference Books, 1998.

Yegul, Fikret. *Baths and Bathing in Classical Antiquity*. Cambridge, MA: MIT Press, 1992.

Text and Image Credits

Location photography shot at the home of John Caner and George Beier, Sonoma, CA, and scouted by Peter Scott Location Scouting, (415) 395-9446.

Location photography props generously donated from Dandelion, 55 Potrero Avenue, San Francisco, CA 94103 (415) 436-9500

and

The Gardener, 1836 Fourth Street, Berkeley, CA 94710 (510) 548-4545.

Excerpt on page 25 from *Celebrating Your New Jewish Daughter: Creating Jewish Ways to Welcome Baby Girls into the Covenant—New and Traditional Ceremonies* © Debra Nussbaum Cohen (Woodstock, VT: Jewish Lights Publishing). Permission granted by Jewish Lights Publishing, P.O. Box 237, Woodstock, VT 05091 www.jewishlights.com

Excerpt on page 70 reprinted by permission from *A Druid's Herbal for the Sacred Earth* by Ellen Evert Hopman, Destiny Books, a division of Inner Traditions International, Rochester, VT 05767. Copyright © by Ellen Evert Hopman.

Excerpt on page 76 reprinted by permission from Sarolta G. DeFaltay, an instructor in ritual and astrology since 1995. For more information, newsletters, and an online correspondence course go to http://moonspells.com.

Excerpt on page 77 reprinted by permission from *The Wicca Cookbook* by Jamie Wood and Tara Seefeldt, Celestial Arts, Berkeley, CA . Copyright © by Jamie Wood and Tara Seefeldt.

Photo Credits

Page 6 © Adam Woolfitt/CORBIS.

Page 16 © 2001 Janice Rubin, the Mikvah Project, www. mikvahproject.com.

Page 32 © Christine Osborne/CORBIS.

Page 34 © Hutchinson Picture Library/Michael Lee.

Page 36 © Gianni Dagli Orti/CORBIS.

Page 43 © The State Russian Museum/CORBIS.

Page 49 © Harald A. Jahn; Viennaslide Photoagency/CORBIS.

Page 50 © Mimmo Jodice/CORBIS.

Page 54 © Jonathan Blair/CORBIS.

Page 56 © Mimmo Jodice/CORBIS.

Page 58 © Perrin Pierre/CORBIS.

Page 68 *Lady of the Waters* © Brian Froud; World of Froud from *The Runes of Elfland* by Brian Froud and Ari Berk, Harry N. Abrams Inc. www.WorldofFroud.com

Page 87 © Mark E. Gibson/CORBIS.

Page 88 © Jan Butchofsky-Houser/CORBIS.

Page 103 © Macduff Everton.

Page 110 © Gianni Dagli Orti/CORBIS.

Page 116 © Julie Houck/CORBIS.

Page 119 © Wolfgang Kaehler/CORBIS.

Page 120 © Craig Lovell/CORBIS.

Page 134 © Michael S. Yamashita/CORBIS.

Page 141 © Dana Levy.

Page 152 © Hulton-Deutsch Collection/CORBIS.

Page 176 © Stapleton Collection/CORBIS